FINANCIALLY REWARDING TERRORISM IN THE WEST BANK

HEARING

BEFORE THE

COMMITTEE ON FOREIGN AFFAIRS
HOUSE OF REPRESENTATIVES

ONE HUNDRED FOURTEENTH CONGRESS

SECOND SESSION

JULY 6, 2016

Serial No. 114–201

Printed for the use of the Committee on Foreign Affairs

Available via the World Wide Web: http://www.foreignaffairs.house.gov/ or
http://www.gpo.gov/fdsys/

U.S. GOVERNMENT PUBLISHING OFFICE

20–651PDF WASHINGTON : 2016

For sale by the Superintendent of Documents, U.S. Government Publishing Office
Internet: bookstore.gpo.gov Phone: toll free (866) 512–1800; DC area (202) 512–1800
Fax: (202) 512–2104 Mail: Stop IDCC, Washington, DC 20402–0001

CONTENTS

FINANCIALLY REWARDING TERRORISM IN THE WEST BANK

WEDNESDAY, JULY 6, 2016

House of Representatives,
Committee on Foreign Affairs,
Washington, DC.

The committee met, pursuant to notice, at 10:13 a.m., in room 2172, Rayburn House Office Building, Hon. Edward Royce (chairman of the committee) presiding.

Chairman ROYCE. This hearing will come to order.

The title of this hearing is "Financially Rewarding Terrorism in the West Bank."

And as everyone here knows, last week, a 13-year-old Israeli-American girl was stabbed to death by a Palestinian terrorist while she slept in her bed. Sadly, Hallel Ariel's murder is only the latest attack in Israel, because since October there have been 250 instances of Israelis being chased down, shot, or stabbed. Forty have died, including former U.S. Army Officer Taylor Force, who was stabbed in March along an oceanfront boardwalk.

While this spree of attacks continues, international diplomats continue to meet for a probable push at the United Nations this fall to impose the "parameters" of peace on Israel and the Palestinian Authority. But what on earth suggests that Israel has a willing partner in peace at this time?

Last fall, this committee held a hearing to expose the Palestinian Authority's complicity in inciting violence. Israel is contending with a deep-seated hatred, nurtured by Palestinian leaders over many years in mosques, in schools, in newspapers, nurtured on television, on radio. As one witness told the committee, " 'Incitement' is the term we usually use, but 'hatred' is what we mean . . . teaching generations of Palestinian children to hate Jews by demonizing and dehumanizing them."

Take the funeral for the killer of American Taylor Force, a former West Point graduate, U.S. Army officer, and Vanderbilt student. Official PA TV glorified the terrorist, calling him "a Martyr" 11 times in the broadcast I watched. A reporter explained that his funeral was a "large national wedding befitting of Martyrs."

But Palestinians are lured to terrorism with more than just words. Since 2003, it has been Palestinian law to reward Palestinian prisoners in Israeli jails with a monthly paycheck—legislation which creates jihad. Under this act, the Palestinian Authority and the Palestinian Liberation Organization use a so-called "martyrs' fund" to pay the families of Palestinian prisoners and suicide bombers. One prominent Palestinian says that these inducements have become "sacred in Palestinian politics."

You know, as a member of one concerned family here today reminded me, these terrorists are not, in fact, lone rangers, they are not lone wolves acting from their independent hatred. Instead, these terrorists are the product of the programming done by the PA's perverted culture that glorifies the willingness to die or to spend time in prison in pursuit of killing or maiming Israelis. The PA programmed this hate. These financial rewards are the main way they accomplish this.

And, perversely, the PA uses a sliding scale: The more the mayhem, the longer the jail sentence, then the greater the financial reward. The highest payments go to those serving life sentences—to those who prove most brutal. And, as we will hear today, the PA allots $140 million of its budget for this purpose. The monthly salary ranges from $364 a month for 3 years' imprisonment to over $3,000 a month for 30 years or more.

And whoever hits the bar, whoever was imprisoned for 5 years or more—and we know what kind of attack would create that—that individual is entitled to permanent employment in what? In the PA institution itself. Again, for those who wage the most brutal attacks. If a Palestinian state was established, it is hard to see how this "pay to slay" policy wouldn't put them on the State Sponsors of Terrorism list today.

With about one-third of the Palestinian Authority's budget financed through foreign aid, the U.S. and our European allies can— and must—help stop the bloodshed. So far, the international community has failed to effectively use its leverage. European donors admit they provide funding in a way that is impossible to track. They have nothing in their laws like the U.S. requirement—which the Israeli Government is now starting to embrace—that funding of the PA be cut by the amount the PA pays out for acts of terrorism. This must change. And if the PA's irresponsible behavior continues, the whole premise for funding the PA needs to be reconsidered.

The U.S. needs to do better at bringing the parties together while holding the parties responsible for their actions. This has traditionally been our role. Unfortunately, in recent years, the Obama administration has been hesitant to hold the PA accountable—yet has consistently pressured Israel.

It is no wonder the Palestinian Authority believes they can go straight to the United Nations this fall, bypassing Israel and bypassing bilateral negotiations. Indeed, the Obama administration has pointedly not ruled out allowing the U.N. Security Council to dictate the terms of peace negotiations. The United States should make it abundantly clear that we oppose such actions which are not based on direct negotiations between the parties and will use our veto and keep divisive, counterproductive resolutions from passing.

We have to face reality if we are going to move peace forward, and we have to be honest about each actor's readiness to make peace. The sad truth is the Palestinian Authority has not prepared its citizens for peace with Israel. Quite the opposite. And, tragically, there will be no peace until that changes.

And I now turn to the ranking member for any opening comments Mr. Eliot Engel of New York may have.

Mr. ENGEL. Thank you, Mr. Chairman, for calling this morning's hearing. The threats facing Israel and the challenges to reaching a two-state solution are growing every day, and I am glad the committee is focusing on this.

I want to thank all our witnesses, as well. Welcome to the Foreign Affairs Committee. We are grateful for your time and your expertise.

I especially want to welcome back former Congressman Robert Wexler, who spent many hours on this side of the dais on the Foreign Affairs Committee sitting next to me. It is good to have you back, Robert.

And thanks to our other witnesses, as well. Thank you for joining us.

Before I start with my statement, I want to offer my condolences to the family of Hallel Yaffa Ariel. She was the young Israel girl, 13 years old, who was stabbed to death in her own bedroom by a 17-year-old Palestinian boy. It is just hard to fathom, but that is what we end up with after years and years of incitement to violence.

The chairman and I have talked about this ad nauseam with the Palestinian leadership. Everyone will hear us. You cannot have incitement and expect to have peace. Young people in classrooms taught to hate a group of people regarded as less than human, this doesn't solve any problems. It is creates new ones, like this disgrace of this poor girl.

Of course, when the Palestinian leadership, whether it be the PLO or the Palestinian Authority, sends money to convicted terrorists and their families, it is no wonder that individuals are incentivized to commit acts of violence. This culture of incitement must end. It is absolutely outrageous to pay cold-blooded killers and call them martyrs. It is just disgraceful. At a time when U.S. money is going to the Palestinian Authority, for them to do this just makes you scratch your head. It is not acceptable, and it is not tolerable, and it won't be tolerated.

Of course, the culture of incitement needs to end because the loss of innocent life is unacceptable, and it must end because violence and terrorism will never lead to a two-state solution. I have repeatedly said to the Palestinians they will never achieve their state on the backs of terrorism—just plain and simple. I believe they are entitled to their state in a two-state solution, but they will never get it if they think terrorism is the way to go.

In my view, a two-state solution is the only way for Israel to remain both a Jewish state and a democracy, but right now a number of roadblocks are keeping that solution out of reach.

First, Israel faces threats on every border. Some of Israel's enemies possess incredibly sophisticated missile systems. Others are lone-wolf terrorists carrying forward the recent wave of violence we have seen. With this feeling of being under siege, the Israeli public's confidence in a peaceful solution continues to erode. What else would you expect? The idea of living side-by-side with their Arab neighbors seems like a remote possibility, and this is precisely what the violent extremists want.

At the same time, Israel faces mounting threats to its physical security. There is a growing effort to undermine Israel's legitimacy. The so-called BDS, Boycott Divestment and Sanctions, movement—shameful and disgraceful, in my opinion—pushes Israel to make unilateral concessions outside direct negotiations with the Palestinians. The BDS movement is totally at odds with a negotiated two-state solution, which, in my opinion, should remain our focus.

So how do we resume progress toward that goal? Frankly, I think gatherings like the Paris peace talks last month are an unhelpful distraction because neither the Israelis nor the Palestinians were involved. How can powers come together and think they will come up with a solution without the two parties at the table? It just doesn't make sense.

The only way to have peace and settle the Palestinian situation is face-to-face talks between Israelis and Palestinians. There can be no imposition of a peace plan from the outside. The U.N. is a farce. Israel cannot get a fair hearing at the U.N. Why should Israel submit itself to such things? Direct negotiations between the parties. And the Palestinians have to understand they have to make concessions.

I point out to people that, in the past couple of decades, there were two times that a two-state solution seemed like a possibility in terms of an agreement: Once in 2001 with Yasser Arafat and then in 2008 with Mahmoud Abbas. Ehud Barak was Prime Minister of Israel, and then Ehud Olmert was Prime Minister of Israel. The Israelis said, yes, they were willing to make painful concessions. And, at the end, ultimately, the Palestinians said no and backed out, because they talked about right of return and all kinds of other roadblocks.

If there were two states and there is a two-state solution, Palestinians get the right of return to the Palestinian state, not to the Israel state, not to the Jewish state. And if the Palestinians want peace, they certainly haven't demonstrated it, in my opinion, at all.

We know what the unresolved issues are: Borders, security, refugees, Jerusalem, and a mutual recognition of the end of the conflict. That would require the Palestinians to recognize Israel as a state for the Jewish people with equal rights for all its citizens, and I believe the Palestinians' refusal to do this is one of the main reasons there is no Palestinian state today.

We also know what the pitfalls are of resuming talks. Every time there is a new initiative, expectations soar, and each time the talks fall apart, things seem to crash a little harder. That outcome leads to violence. Extremists find a louder voice, and people on both sides suffer. And it is interesting, every time it seems like there might be some kind of an agreement, you have violent terrorism to try to destroy it, because the terrorists don't want peace. They want to keep the pot stirring.

Just look in Gaza, where Hamas has tightened its grip over the last decade. And let's remember that Hamas is a terrorist organization. Reconstruction is slowly progressing. Israel has expanded the fishing perimeter in the Mediterranean, granted thousands of work permits, and improved access to telecom technology. What has Hamas done? Rebuilt its terror tunnel network—and the chairman and I were there in those tunnels, and so we saw firsthand what

Hamas builds—and periodically fire rockets and missiles into Israel, terrorizing innocent people, forcing them to run for their lives to the nearest shelter.

In this context, I want to voice my support for a new long-term memorandum of understanding, an MOU, between the U.S. and Israel. We want to stop this horrific violence, but as long as Israel faces these threats, we need to stand with them and help ensure their defense and security. I urge the administration to bend over backwards to negotiate an MOU with Israel that will let Israel keep its qualitative military edge and strengthen Israel against all these threats that it faces from terrorists.

So I will wrap up by saying there aren't any easy answers. And, to our witnesses, we are glad to have your voices in the mix. I look forward to your testimony. And, again, as the chairman said, I agree with what he said; it is just outrageous to pay cold-blooded killers who murder innocent civilians and call them martyrs. I cannot think of anything more disgusting.

So I look forward to the testimony of our witnesses, and I yield back.

Chairman ROYCE. Thank you.

This morning, we are pleased to be joined by a distinguished panel.

We have Dr. David Pollock, Kaufman Fellow at the Washington Institute for Near East Policy. And, previously, Dr. Pollock served as a senior adviser for the broader Middle East at the State Department.

Mr. Yigal Carmon is president and founder of the Middle East Media Research Institute. Prior to founding this organization, he was a counterterrorism adviser to two Israeli Prime Ministers.

The Honorable Robert Wexler is President of the S. Daniel Abraham Center for Middle East Peace. Previously, Congressman Wexler served as a member of this committee and served in the House of Representatives from 1997 to 2010. He represented Florida's 19th District. We welcome him back to the committee.

And so, without objection, the witnesses' full prepared statements will be made part of the record.

Members here will have 5 calendar days to submit any statements or any questions of our witnesses or any extraneous material for the record.

And we will start with Dr. David Pollock.

STATEMENT OF DAVID POLLOCK, PH.D., KAUFMAN FELLOW, WASHINGTON INSTITUTE FOR NEAR EAST POLICY

Mr. POLLOCK. Thank you very much, Mr. Chairman, Ranking Member, honorable colleagues, and distinguished fellow speakers, for this opportunity to meet with you today. I am truly honored by it, and I greatly appreciate both this very prestigious forum and the significance of the issue at hand.

But I believe if there is one thing that most Americans, Israelis, and Arabs would agree on today, it is that the Israeli-Palestinian conflict right now is not the most important or the most urgent conflict in the Middle East or for U.S. foreign policy.

And, for that reason, I would argue that now is precisely the wrong time to put the Israeli-Palestinian issue near the top of our foreign policy priorities. And, also, I would argue that certain current ideas about doing that, about putting this issue at the top of our priorities, carry a very real, albeit unwitting, risk of doing more harm than good.

I agree with the statement of the chairman and of the ranking member that multilateral diplomatic maneuvers, whether in Paris or at the United Nations, have one central and inescapable flaw. By definition, they encourage one or both parties to imagine that they can somehow avoid making compromises and, ultimately, peace with each other.

This is not merely a matter of avoiding direct Israeli-Palestinian bilateral negotiations. It is also a matter of avoiding responsibility for the indispensable compromises that would make real peace possible. And that is why, simply put, the Palestinian Authority has become so enamored of this shortcut, or escape hatch, over the past several years.

Doing multilateral initiatives in the absence of direct negotiations is not, as is sometimes said, better than nothing. It is, in fact, worse than nothing, because it actually helps prevent rather than promote peace.

Now, what I would like to do in the few minutes that I have left is to focus on what I believe would be some more constructive steps, to look forward rather than backward.

First and most urgently, I believe the United States should enhance its support for Israeli-Palestinian security cooperation. Despite all of the incitement coming from the Palestinian Authority, security cooperation with Israel continues, and this is the bedrock of any work to stabilize the situation and ultimately reconcile the parties. The United States supports this effort, and that support, I believe, should not only continue but intensify.

Second, as my colleague Dennis Ross has written recently and as I wrote at the Washington Institute as far back as 2008, I think the United States should revive a deal with Israel about limiting settlement activity, roughly along the lines of the Bush-Sharon letter and related understandings of 2005. Israel could announce that it will cease new construction beyond the security barrier, or just act in that fashion without a declaration, in return for a U.S. commitment to cease criticizing that settlement construction—that limited settlement construction.

Third, the U.S. should quietly encourage Israel and the Palestinians to agree on new practical forms of economic cooperation and of people-to-people interaction, including interfaith Jewish-Muslim dialogue. The more these people-to-people projects can be scaled up, the more they are likely to make a positive difference.

There is currently a bipartisan bill, H.R. 1489, to create an international fund for precisely that purpose. I respectfully urge you to give this bill your full support, in the firm conviction that it will pay multiple dividends in the coming years.

Fourth, the United States should actively explore new ideas for enlisting Arab backing for Israeli-Palestinian peace.

Fifth, and finally, the United States should publicly support and very vocally encourage others to endorse what we used to call mutual and balanced but, if necessary, unilateral steps toward peaceful coexistence.

Israel, for example, could stop the demolition of Palestinian buildings. The Palestinian Authority could stop referring to murderers as ''martyrs.'' The Palestinian Authority and Israel could endorse new programs of interfaith dialogue to advance tolerance, nonviolence, and peaceful coexistence, and so on. I would be happy during the question-and-answer period to expand on these and other specific, I hope constructive ideas.

With that, I offer my sincere thanks once again to the committee and to you, Mr. Chairman, for this opportunity to share my thoughts on this important topic. Thank you.

[The prepared statement of Mr. Pollock follows:]

Written Statement of Dr. David Pollock
Kaufman Senior Fellow and Director, Fikra Forum
The Washington Institute for Near East Policy
House Committee on Foreign Affairs
Hearing on "Financially Rewarding Terrorism in the West Bank"
July 6, 2016

Thank you very much, Mr. Chairman, Ranking Member, honorable colleagues and distinguished fellow speakers for this opportunity to meet with you today. I am truly honored by it, and I greatly appreciate both this very prestigious forum and the significance of the issue at hand.

As I see it, our primary task here is not to debate the underlying issues of the Israeli-Palestinian conflict, or of past U.S. policy in that regard. Rather, we should focus mainly on these two narrower questions: Is now a good time for major U.S. or other initiatives on that perennial problem? And if not, how can we best help preserve the possibilities of a more constructive approach to the Israeli-Palestinian problem it at some future time?

It is a cliché, but nonetheless true, that the original guiding principle of any serious endeavor should always be, "First, do no harm." Of course, in the real world of politics and diplomacy, nothing is ever certain; so one must weigh the risks of doing harm against the uncertain prospects of doing good. Thus it may be that, in a different era in which the Israeli-Palestinian conflict was more central to regional and even global issues, a risky but potentially productive diplomatic "Hail Mary pass" might have been worthwhile.

But that is simply not the case today. This conflict is now a marginal one, even from the Arab standpoint, and certainly from the American one. It is nowhere near as acute or as consequential, even in the Middle East, as the conflicts against ISIL or among sects and ethnic groups in nearby Syria, Iraq, Turkey, Lebanon, Egypt and beyond. And it is vital to note that, contrary to common misconception, all those conflicts have almost nothing to do with the Israeli-Palestinian one.

Therefore, today it is not just that we should pay more urgent attention to those other conflicts rather than to the Israeli-Palestinian one. Today we must also recognize that even solving, let alone addressing, the Israeli-Palestinian conflict will do almost nothing to resolve or mitigate any other major international problem. And so we must also recognize that the significant risks of failure, backlash, or inadvertent complications caused by an untimely or overly ambitious attempt to deal with Israeli-Palestinian disputes are simply not worth the effort, when much worse and more dangerous conflicts in the region confront us all every day.

Let me be clear. I am not arguing that we should ignore the Israeli-Palestinian conflict. Or that it is unimportant, or unsolvable. But I am arguing that now is precisely the wrong time to put it near the top our foreign policy priorities. And that certain current ideas about doing precisely that carry a very real albeit unwitting risk of doing more harm than good.

What are those well-intentioned but misguided ideas for U.S. policy? There are more than a few in circulation; but I see three seemingly plausible, if actually self-defeating, ones: first, supporting multilateral diplomatic maneuvers like the French initiative, or a new UNSC resolution on the Israeli-Palestinian issue; second, proclaiming a new set of unilateral American ideas or "parameters" about a two-state solution; and third, encouraging or tolerating various forms of pressure on the parties--such as aid cutoffs or economic boycotts--ostensibly as a means of forcing either a change of government or a change of policy. Let me very briefly explain why I think all three would be self-defeating, and then suggest what I believe would be a more constructive approach.

Multilateral diplomatic maneuvers, whether in Paris or at the UNSC, have one central and inescapable flaw: by definition, they encourage one or both parties to imagine that they can somehow avoid making compromises and ultimately peace with each other. This is not merely a matter, as is usually thought, of avoiding direct Israeli-Palestinian bilateral negotiations. It is also a matter of avoiding responsibility for the indispensable compromises that would make real peace possible: whether on borders, on refugees, on incitement, on settlements, on Jerusalem, on mutual recognition, or on finally ending the conflict and any associated claims.

That is why, simply put, the Palestinian Authority has become so enamored of this "shortcut" or "escape hatch" over the past several years. And that is why, especially in the absence of direct negotiations, a multilateral initiative of this kind is not, as is too often said, "better than nothing." It is in fact worse than nothing, because it actually helps prevent rather than promote peace.

To be sure, once the parties do engage in genuine give and take, there would be a very useful role for international diplomatic intervention. It could help bridge gaps between Israeli and Palestinian negotiating positions, provide valuable additional inputs in the form of security and economic incentives, and expand the circle of peace to include an important renewed regional dimension. Possibly a multilateral framework could even come up with creative new ideas for formulating and implementing an eventual peace agreement, perhaps in transitional stages.

But all that must await a clear demonstration by both parties that they are ready for real bargaining–or else the multilateral route risks hardening positions, raising false expectations, and repeating failure. And at this point, repeated failure could well be the last straw in tipping the balance toward an almost irreversible conviction, on both sides, that peace and a two-state solution are simply not possible.

Nevertheless, in defense of this multilateral mirage, one sometimes hears the refrain that "twenty years of Oslo negotiations have yielded nothing, so it's time to try something different." Nonsense. If not for Oslo, there would be no Palestinian Authority, no historic steps toward mutual recognition, no Palestinian self-rule anywhere, no peace between Israel and Jordan, and probably no end of Israel's occupation in Gaza. On balance, with all of their shortcomings, this represents progress. And that progress has stalled not due to Oslo or to inconclusive direct peace talks but to their opposite: the second intifadah, the resulting disillusionment in Israel, and most recently the PA's decision to abandon negotiations in favor of the fruitless quest for an internationally "imposed" settlement on its own terms.

The two other misguided alternatives to direct peace talks can be dispensed with very briefly, because they both suffer from the same fatal flaws outlined above. In addition, as my Arab colleague and friend Ghaith al-Omari has lately written, both a new UNSC resolution, or an American presidential "parameters" speech or similar policy departure, are more likely than not to be rejected by both parties as insufficient or unacceptable. Obviously they would do so for different reasons, but the effect would be the same: another costly and counter-productive failure.

Last in this series of self-defeating proposals comes the notion of pressuring the parties (usually meaning Israel) to change their government or at least their policies. This too is, I believe, also mostly a mirage. For one thing, to reiterate my main objection, outside pressure on one side only tempts the other side to harden its position, placing compromise out of reach. That is not peculiar to these parties; it is human nature.

For another thing, the U.S. and others have already wasted far too much time and effort trying to engineer a change in Israel's leadership or coalition government. We or others may now be contemplating a parallel "remote-control" effort on the Palestinian side, as Mahmoud Abbas seems increasingly to be losing his grip on power, or at least popularity. Yet the record shows that this is almost always a fool's errand. In reality, each party will have to choose its own leader. And they will have to convince each other to compromise, if that is indeed what they want. Outsiders can perhaps "nudge" them in that direction, to use a faddish term, but the main onus, and opportunity, lies with the Israelis and the Palestinians themselves.

So, what more constructive "nudges" should we contemplate? Allow me to suggest a short list of them for your consideration.

First, and most urgently, the U.S. should enhance its support for Israeli-Palestinian security cooperation. This is the bedrock of any work to stabilize the situation and ultimately reconcile the parties. I defer to LTG Rudesheim, who is so capably leading this essential mission on the ground today, regarding details. Suffice it for me to mention my own view that the U.S. should discreetly encourage both sides to further expand their recent tacit understandings about limiting Israeli incursions into Area A, and look toward increasing PA security activities in Area B--and possibly even in Palestinian neighborhoods of East Jerusalem outside the wall, which have become a sort of no man's land of crime and violence.

Second, as my colleague Dennis Ross has written recently, and as I wrote at the Washington Institute as far back as 2008, the U.S. should revive a deal with Israel about limiting settlement activity--roughly along the lines of the Bush-Sharon letter and related understandings of 2005. Israel could announce that it will cease new construction beyond the security barrier, or just act consistently in that fashion, in return for a U.S. commitment to cease criticizing that construction. This would immediately benefit both U.S.-Israeli and Palestinian-Israeli relations, even if the PA does not publicly register its approval. And for the longer term, it would help preserve the possibility of a two-state solution some day.

Third, the U.S. should quietly encourage Israel and the Palestinians to agree on new practical form of economic cooperation, and of people-to-people interaction. In particular, without sacrificing security or political bargaining positions, they could greatly upgrade the scope of Palestinian construction and other business activity in Area C, for which international investment would be readily available. This is not about the false promise of "economic peace," which I realize is not a substitute for political agreements. Rather, it would be a good-faith, short-term measure to improve the objective situation, and the subjective atmosphere, for people on both sides, pending more fundamental positive changes and hopefully also leading in that direction. And it would correspond to the expressed wishes of the local Palestinian population, who despite the siren call of BDS overwhelmingly tell Palestinian pollsters that they want more, not less, Israeli jobs, investment, and overall economic interaction.

In this context, the PA's equivocal encouragement of "anti-normalization" campaigns is a serious and completely counterproductive barrier to peace. Despite this obstacle, there are many brave souls and competent NGO leaders, on both sides, who continue to work together on social coexistence and cooperation projects. They need and richly deserve our intensified support, especially at this time when high-level political efforts are stymied. I would even go further, and say that these people-to-people programs are among the very best long-term investments we can all make in promoting the possibility of peace. This is much more than just feel-good symbolism; it really matters, and it really works. It worked in Northern Ireland, in Rwanda, and elsewhere, where it proved to be a crucial missing link in resolving equally bloody and entrenched ethnic or sectarian conflicts.

The more these people-to-people projects can be scaled up, the more they are likely to make a major positive difference. There is currently a bipartisan bill, HR 1489, to create an International Fund for precisely that purpose. I respectfully urge you to give this bill your full support, in the firm conviction that it will pay multiple dividends in the coming years.

Fourth, the U.S. should actively explore new ideas for enlisting Arab backing for Israeli-Palestinian peace. I understand that some of the hype about "pragmatic Sunnis," or about Arab-Israeli "strategic convergence" against the common enemies of Iran and terrorism, is exaggerated. Still, there is something here to build upon. The U.S. should prevail upon the Arab League, for instance, to reaffirm that the Arab Peace Initiative allows for land swaps, rather than insisting literally on the 1967 boundaries. And we should press for a more explicit or even formal statement that the API could be negotiated and implemented in phases, alongside progress on the Palestinian front, rather than as a "take it or leave it" aftermath of a final Israeli-Palestinian accord.

Fifth, and finally, the U.S. should publicly support, and very vocally encourage others to endorse, what we used to call "mutual and balanced" but if necessary unilateral steps toward peaceful coexistence. For example:

If Israel stops demolition of Palestinian buildings, then the U.S. should applaud that decision and spearhead some form of international acknowledgement of it, in the Quartet, UN, or other appropriate forum.

If the PA stops referring to murderers as "martyrs," then the U.S. should applaud that decision and spearhead an appropriate international acknowledgment of it.

If either the PA or Israel, and preferably both, endorse new programs of interfaith dialogue to advance tolerance, non-violence, and peaceful coexistence, then the U.S. should warmly welcome those initiatives and mobilize broader international support for them, including from our many Muslim friends. Such courageous voices from the inside are the best antidote to the religious extremism that so concerns all of us these days.

fIf other countries recognize a Palestinian state, then the U.S. should encourage them to accept the logical conclusion: Palestinian refugees are no longer stateless, so their "right of return" applies not to Israel but to Palestine.

If the U.S. agrees that Jerusalem should be the capital of a Palestinian state, then the U.S. should recognize Jerusalem as the capital of Israel. In fact, unbeknownst to most experts, even the UN has already made a major stride in this positive direction: the same UNGA resolution that admits Palestine as an observer also officially asserts that Jerusalem should be the capital both of Palestine and of Israel.

If Israel allows more Turkish and other international humanitarian and reconstruction aid into Gaza, then the U.S. should not only applaud that decision, but also work with third-party monitors to ensure the aid is not diverted by Hamas to build tunnels, missiles, or other weapons of war.

And if the PA recognizes Israel as a state for the Jewish people, or at least drops its objection to Arab steps toward that goal, then the U.S. should not only applaud that decision, but also press Israel to make good on Prime Minister Netanyahu's earlier proclamation that this "would change everything" – presumably for the better.

The preceding list is naturally just illustrative, not exhaustive, and I would of course welcome additions or friendly amendments to it. I offer it for your consideration in the firm conviction that it offers better alternatives than two others that I noted in my introduction: either trying to do too much to solve the Israeli-Palestinian conflict, or failing to do enough.

With that I offer my sincere thanks once again to the Committee and to you, Mr. Chairman, for this opportunity to share my thoughts on this important topic. With great respect, I look forward to your questions, suggestions, and discussion.

———————

Chairman ROYCE. Mr. Carmon.

STATEMENT OF MR. YIGAL CARMON, PRESIDENT AND FOUNDER, MIDDLE EAST MEDIA RESEARCH INSTITUTE

Mr. CARMON. Thank you, Mr. Chairman, Ranking Member, members of the committee.

My testimony is dedicated to the financial support given by the Palestinian Authority to prisoners and to families of martyrs who continued their terrorist activities after the Oslo Accord of 1993, in which Arafat committed on behalf of the Palestinian people to end all forms of terrorism and, by that commitment, won recognition among nations.

By providing this support at the amount of $300 million per year, the PLO violates Oslo, encourages terrorism. And by using, or misusing, actually, the money of donor countries, including the United States, it makes them unwittingly complicit to this act of supporting terrorism.

Let me deal with the details of this support. The PA distributes the money through two bodies of the PLO. One is the Palestinian National Fund, which deals with the prisoners and distributes the money through another Commission for Detainees, and the other is the Institute for the Caring of Families of Martyrs.

This support for prisoners is anchored in a series of laws but chiefly Law No. 14 and Law No. 19 of 2004 and Law No. 1 of 2013. The law describes the prisoners as a fighting sector whose rights and the rights of their families must be assured without discrimination.

What do these words mean? They mean that Hamas terrorists and Islamic jihad, PFLP, others, like a squad that bombed the cafeteria of the Hebrew U. 9 years after Oslo, in which four Americans were killed, will get support, like the killers of Taylor Force and their families. I hold in my hand documents which I hope to include in the testimony—we got them this morning—which demonstrate from PA official documents that they get this support.

What are they entitled to? They get salaries, jobs, exemptions in education, health care, and more. Years in jails are calculated as years of seniority in government service, and priority in jobs are given to those who are personally involved in acts of terrorism.

The annual amount reaches $140 million. And the implementation of the laws is through a series of decisions by the PA Government, particularly Decision 23 of 2010, which set the levels of salaries. As you had mentioned, Mr. Chairman, it is $364 per month to those who were sentenced to 3 years, up to $3,120 to those who were sentenced to 30 years for more brutal acts. There is a special supplement for Jerusalemites of $78 per month and for Israeli Arabs at the level of $130 per month above the regular salary.

They also get the money for the canteen in jail at the level of no less than $780,000 per year.

At times when there is tension between the PA and the other organizations, President Abbas doesn't hesitate to cut them down, cut the salaries down. More on that you will find in my written testimony.

Let me move to the issue of the families of martyrs. The general amount is $173 million per year. And these are distributed not by any specific law but by the laws that dominate social affairs, the conditions of the family and so on.

But here again, it is—these two magic words—without discrimination. Namely, President Abbas and the PA claim to follow a peaceful political path, different than that of the other Palestinian organizations who followed the path of armed struggle and jihad. But, at the same time, they fund all those who follow the terrorists' violent path. It is not just about the incitement to violence; it is about funding it. It is about guaranteeing an environment supportive of terror.

In conclusion, one can understand the PLO's commitment to support families of martyrs in the era before Oslo in the context of an overall peaceful reconciliation. But the fact that the PA supports those who continue terrorist activity after Oslo for many years now using donor countries' money is a basic violation of the Oslo Accords and a deliberate encouragement of terrorism. This is a situation the donor countries never meant or wanted, and it is in their hands to put an end to it.

Mr. Chairman, much more details are in my written testimony. I wish to thank you again for this opportunity to present the facts of this report.

[The prepared statement of Mr. Carmon follows:]

Palestinian Authority Support for Imprisoned, Released and Wounded Terrorists and Families of 'Martyrs'

Written testimony submitted to the House Committee on Foreign Affairs, for "Financially Rewarding Terrorism in the West Bank," July 6, 2016.

Yigal Carmon, President and Founder, The Middle East Media Research Institute (MEMRI), Washington, D.C.

Mr. Chairman, Ranking Members, and Members of the Committee,

My testimony today is dedicated to a persistent problem: the financial and other support given by the Palestinian Authority (PA) to those who have continued their terrorist activities after the Oslo Accords, in which Yasser Arafat made a commitment, on behalf of the Palestinian people, to stop all terrorist activity.

By providing this support, the PA is encouraging terrorism in violation of its Oslo commitment.

Furthermore, the PA has been using money granted by donor countries for this purpose, and by doing so, has made them complicit in encouraging terrorism as well.

The details of this support, which I will cite in my testimony, may sound somewhat tedious, and I apologize for this in advance. They are taken both from the Palestinian media and from official PA records, available online.

MEMRI, as you may know, has been monitoring and analyzing the Middle East media for nearly 20 years. My testimony today is based not only on an analysis of the PA 2016 budget, but on years of research.

Details of the PA Support for Terrorists
The PA transfers the funds through two PLO organizations:

- The National Palestinian Fund, which transfers moneys for the prisoners and released prisoners (further to be disbursed by the Commission for Detainees and Ex-Detainees Affairs)
- The Institute for Care for the Families of Martyrs, which transfers moneys for the families of martyrs.

This financial support for prisoners is anchored in a series of laws and government decrees, chiefly Laws No. 14 and No. 19 of 2004, and Law No. 1 of 2013.[1] The prisoners are described as "a fighting sector and an integral part of the weave of Arab Palestinian society" and it is stated that "the financial rights of the prisoner and his family" must be assured. It is also stated that the PA will provide the allowance to "every prisoner, without discrimination."

According to the laws, the PA must provide prisoners with a monthly allowance during their incarceration and salaries or jobs upon their release. They are also entitled to exemptions from payments for education, health care, and professional training. Their years of imprisonment are calculated as years of seniority of service in PA institutions. It should be noted that whoever was imprisoned for five years or more is entitled to a job in a PA institution. Thus, the PA gives priority in job placement to people who were involved in terrorist activity.

Palestinian President Mahmoud 'Abbas has stressed more than once that "the prisoners are top priority."[2] As a result of this commitment, the PA invests significant sums in underwriting the expenses of the prisoners and their families - $137.8 million according to the PA's 2016 budget (about 7% of which is for officials' salaries and operating expenses) (see Appendix, Figure 1).[3] Over the years, the Palestinian government has taken a series of decisions implementing the laws.[4]

The allowances are currently paid based on PA Government Decision No. 23 of 2010, which specifies the prisoners' monthly allowance according to length of sentence. It ranges from $364 a month for up to three years imprisonment to $3,120 for 30 years and more. There is a $78 supplement for terrorists from Jerusalem and a $130 supplement for Arab Israeli terrorists. (For the full chart, see Appendix, Figure 2):[5]

The PA also provides prisoners with a monthly allowance for canteen expenses, totaling $780,000 per month.[6]

Although the law states that prisoners should be given allowances "without discrimination," sometimes the PA has cut allowances for political reasons. For example, in December 2015, allowances were cut from $338 to $208 for released prisoners who are members of Hamas and the Islamic Jihad, and, recently, for members of the PFLP as well, following political tension between these organizations and the PA.[7]

This political decision aroused the protest of the director of the Commission for Detainees and Ex-Detainees Affairs, 'Issa Qaraqe', who said that "it is unacceptable for the Ministry of Finance to cut a prisoner's salary."[8] His statement proves two things: that it is the PA that is funding these allowances and that the PA can and does cut allowances to prisoners when it wishes.

In May 2014, an administrative change took place
'Abbas issued a presidential order according to which the payments to prisoners would no longer be made by the PA's Ministry of Prisoners' Affairs. Instead, they would be disbursed by a PLO Commission for Detainees and Ex-Detainees Affairs.

The aim of this deliberately misleading move was to alleviate pressure on the PA by donor countries that do not wish their money to be channeled to support terrorism. However, the offices remained the same and the official in charge remained the same under a new job title. The source of the money remains the PA, which receives them from donor countries, and the overseeing body remains none other than the PA.

Several high-ranking Palestinian officials have addressed this change:
In June 2014, the former Deputy Minister for Prisoners' Affairs, Ziyad Abu 'Ayn, explained that "the national interest requires" this change because the donor countries "have established dozens of investigative committees focusing on the issue of [their] funds that are transferred from the PA to the prisoners."[9]

PA officials have admitted that the PA remains the financer and the decision-maker in all things pertaining to support for the prisoners and the martyrs' families.

For example, in September 2014, the director for detainees and ex-detainees affairs in Hebron, Ibrahim Najajra, said that the change of status from ministry to commission "would not detract from the prisoners' value or from their legal, moral, or political status, since the services extended to them are anchored in law." He added that the commission would be under the direct supervision of the Palestinian presidency, and that the payments would be made directly by the PLO's National Palestinian Fund.[10]

In December 2015, PA Cabinet Secretary 'Ali Abu Diyak announced that the PA government was committed to continuing to pay allowances to fighters imprisoned for their national struggle and to the families of the martyrs, the wounded, and the prisoners.[11]

Let me move to the PA support for families of "martyrs"
The 2016 budget describes the PLO's Institute for Care for the Families of Martyrs as the body "responsible for ensuring a dignified life to the families of all those martyred and wounded as a result of being participants or bystanders in the revolution."

It is allocated just under $173 million ($172,534,733) for families of martyrs and the wounded within the homeland and outside it. The Institute's operating expenses comes to about $1.5 million. (See Appendix, Figure 3).

The budget also states that the Institute provides allowances "without discrimination" – in other words, also from Hamas, Islamic Jihad, and so on.[12]

Palestinian Prime Minister Rami Hamdallah said recently, on June 17, 2016, that "the government will continue to act together with the PLO institutions to improve the allowances of the families of the martyrs as soon as possible."[13]

What are the details of the payments to the families of the martyrs?
According to reports from 2011 in the Palestinian media, the family of every "martyr" receives a one-time payment of $1,560, as well as a monthly allowance of $364. There are also additional payments based on various criteria, including family status – the family of a married martyr receives an additional $104, and if he has children, the family receives $52 per child[14] – whether the martyr was a civilian or a member of the PA military force, and on his or her rank. (For some of the criteria, see Appendix, Figures 4, 5).

In Conclusion
Let me stress again that as in the case of the support for prisoners, support for the families of martyrs who committed their acts prior to the signing of the Oslo Accords and the PLO commitment to end all forms of terrorism could perhaps be understandable in the context of an overall reconciliation process.

However, the fact that such payments are also given to families of people from various organizations who continue to commit acts of terrorism in violation of the peace accord constitutes deliberate encouragement of terrorism. Consequently, money that originates from donor countries and is used for this purpose makes these countries complicit in the encouragement of terrorism.

APPENDIX

Fig. 1: PA payments to prisoners (in NIS) – 2016 Budget[15]

برنامج: برنامج حماية و رعاية الأسرى و أسرهم و دعم و تأهيل الأسرى المحررين
تكلفة الموازنة التشغيلية والرأسمالية 2016

بند الموازنة	الاسم	موازنة 2016
رواتب وأجور		36802.280
211	الرواتب والاجور	36.802.280
مصاريف تشغيلية		5165.411
221	السفر والمهمات الرسمية	400.000
222	النفقات التشغيلية	1.690.000
223	إيجارات	1.200.000
224	أخرى (تشغيلية)	510.000
225	بدل تنقل	1.265.411
226	مكافآت للموظفين	100.000
مصاريف تحويلية		488371.806
212	المساهمات الاجتماعية	2.371.806
272	منافع المساعدات الاجتماعية	486.000.000
مصاريف رأسمالية		200.000
311	الاصول الثابتة	200.000
اجمالي		530539.497

Fig. 2: Monthly allowances for prisoners (in NIS) – PA Government Decision No. 23, 2010[16]

مـادة (12)

الصرف وفقاً للجدول

يتم صرف الرواتب للأسير استناداً للسنوات التي أمضاها في الأسر وفقاً للجدول التالي :

علاوة أسرى الداخل	علاوة القدس بالشيكل	علاوة الأبناء حتى سن 18 سنة بالشيكل	علاوة الزوجة بالشيكل	الراتب الأساسي بالشيكل	عدد سنوات الأسر
500	300	50 لكل ابن / ابنة	300	1400	من بدء الأسر وأقل من 3 سنوات
500	300	50 لكل ابن / ابنة	300	2000	من 3 سنوات وأقل من 5 سنوات
500	300	50 لكل ابن / ابنة	300	4000	من 5 سنوات وأقل من 10 سنة
500	300	50 لكل ابن / ابنة	300	6000	من 10 سنة وأقل من 15 سنة
500	300	50 لكل ابن / ابنة	300	7000	من 15 سنة وأقل من 20 سنة
500	300	50 لكل ابن / ابنة	300	8000	من 20 سنة وأقل من 25 سنة
500	300	50 لكل ابن / ابنة	300	10000	من 25 سنة وأقل من 30 سنة
500	300	50 لكل ابن / ابنة	300	12000	من 30 سنة فما فوق

Fig. 3: Budget of the Institute for Care for the Families of Martyrs for 2016 (in NIS)[17]

State of Palestine
Ministry of Finance& Planning
Directorate General of Budget

دولة فلسطين
وزارة المالية والتخطيط
الإدارة العامة للموازنة العامة

أبعاد الموازنة للوزارة للسنة المالية 2016

	موازنة مؤسسة رعاية اسر الشهداء		الوزارة / مؤسسة	رقم الموازنة	
إجمالي	برنامج 4403	برنامج 4402	الاسم		
5,735.000	2,685.697	3,049.303	الرواتب والأجور	211	رواتب وأجور
590.448	590.448		النفقات التشغيلية	222	مصاريف تشغيلية
460.000	460.000		إيجارات	223	
100.000	100.000		أخرى (تشغيلية)	224	
381.552	151.499	230.053	بدل تنقل	225	
50.000	50.000		مكافآت للموظفين	226	
594.000	278.228	315.772	المساهمات الاجتماعية	212	مصاريف تحويلية
660,000.000		660,000.000	منافع المساعدات الاجتماعية	272	
50.000	50.000		مخزون	312	مصاريف رأسمالية
667,961.000	4,365.872	663,595.128	إجمالي		
حماية ورعاية وتمكين اسر الشهداء والجرحى داخل الوطن وخارجه				4402	أسماء البرامج
البرنامج الإداري لمؤسسة رعاية اسر الشهداء والجرحى				4403	

Fig. 4: Allowance for families of martyrs, by family status (in NIS) [18]

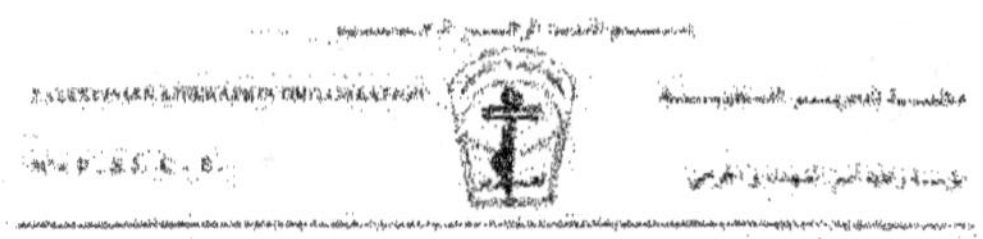

Fi5. 5: Allowance for families of martyrs, by military rank (in NIS)[19]

24

Endnotes:

[1] For Law No. 14 of 2004, see: http://muqtafi.birzeit.edu/pg/getleg.asp?id=14741;
for Law No. 19 of 2004, see: http://muqtafi.birzeit.edu/pg/getleg.asp?id=14777; for Law No. 1 of 2013, see
http://muqtafi.birzeit.edu/pg/getleg.asp?id=16458.

[2] See for example http://www.wafa.ps, February 21, 2005; *Al-Rai* (Jordan), April 28, 2013; www.shasha.ps, April
27, 2013.

[3] For the budget, see: http://www.pmof.ps/documents/10192/654283/BUDGET+BOOK+2016.06.22.pdf/1b8b37ef-
fe73-4ea8-80b3-2ab3bd8c3c68, pp. 753-760.

[4] See for example Government Decision No. 19 of 2010, http://muqtafi.birzeit.edu/pg/getleg.asp?id=16255;
Government Decision No. 21 of 2010, http://muqtafi.birzeit.edu/pg/getleg.asp?id=16257; Government Decision
No. 22 of 2010 http://muqtafi.birzeit.edu/pg/getleg.asp?id=16258; Government Decision No. 23 of 2010,
http://muqtafi.birzeit.edu/pg/getleg.asp?id=16259; Government Decision No. 15 of 2013,
http://muqtafi.birzeit.edu/pg/getleg.asp?id=16556.

[5] *Al-Waqi' Al-Filastiniyya*, Issue No. 90, March 30, 2011, p. 106.

[6] http://maannews.net, September 9, 2014.

[7] *Al-Resala* (Gaza) December 15, 2015.   http://pnn.ps, April 14, 2016.

[8] www.paltimes.net, December 9, 2015.

[9] http://www.eqtesadia.ps, June 4, 2014.

[10] http://hr.ps/ar, September 1, 2014.

[11] http://feneeqnews.com, December 9, 2015. For the budget, see:

[12] For the budget, see:
http://www.pmof.ps/documents/10192/654283/BUDGET+BOOK+2016.06.22.pdf/1b8b37ef-fe73-4ea8-80b3-
2ab3bd8c3c68, pp. 729-736.

[13] http://www.palestinecabinet.gov.ps/WebSite/AR/ViewDetails?ID=37799.

[14] http://www.lajeen-db.ps, August 9, 2011.

[15] http://www.pmof.ps/documents/10192/654283/BUDGET+BOOK+2016.06.22.pdf/1b8b37ef-fe73-4ea8-80b3-
2ab3bd8c3c68, p. 760.

[16] *Al-Waqi' Al-Filastiniyya*, Issue No. 90, March 30, 2011, p. 106.

[17] http://www.pmof.ps/documents/10192/654283/BUDGET+BOOK+2016.06.22.pdf/1b8b37ef-fe73-4ea8-80b3-
2ab3bd8c3c68, p. 735.

[18] https://www.aman-palestine.org/data/itemfiles/b3dd98a029db76be614d1a64dd10604e.pdf, p. 16.

[19] https://www.aman-palestine.org/data/itemfiles/b3dd98a029db76be614d1a64dd10604e.pdf, p. 17.

Chairman ROYCE. Thank you, Mr. Carmon.
Mr. Robert Wexler.

STATEMENT OF THE HONORABLE ROBERT WEXLER, PRESIDENT, S. DANIEL ABRAHAM CENTER FOR MIDDLE EAST PEACE

Mr. WEXLER. Chairman Royce, Ranking Member Engel, members of the committee, thank you very much for your warm welcome.

Israel is often coined the "Start-Up Nation," highlighting the Jewish State's economic miracle and technological and scientific achievements. Just as remarkable is another defining characteristic: Against all odds, Israeli military forces have successfully defended against an onslaught of hostile forces since 1948.

For those of us who are Zionists, the unprecedented security collaboration between the United States and Israel is a source of tremendous pride. The joint development of missile defense technologies, all-time-high intelligence-sharing, historic military training exercises, and the recent delivery of the F-35 Joint Strike Fighter all demonstrate the unbreakable bond between us and Israel.

American administrations and Congress after Congress have ensured Israel's qualitative military advantage. Israel's defense and intelligence coordination with Egypt and Jordan is unprecedented.

Despite these positive developments, the Middle East Quartet report that was released last week asserted that the policies of both Israelis and Palestinians have distanced a two-state outcome, creating a dynamic in which a one-state reality has taken root.

The Quartet calls on the Palestinian Authority to stop incitement of violence, bolster efforts to prevent terrorism, and, importantly, condemn attacks against Israelis. Likewise, the Quartet calls on Israel to cease settlement expansion, transfer civilian authority to the PA in Area C of the West Bank, and bluntly questions Israel's long-term intentions.

With this backdrop of despair and lack of trust on both sides, a stunning development has occurred. The most compelling group now advocating for a two-state solution is the Israel security establishment.

Two weeks ago, a group of over 200 retired generals or equivalent rank from the Israeli Defense Forces, Mossad, Shin Bet, and Israel Police redirected the political discourse. Boldly, Israel's most patriotic soldiers cast aside the question of whether Israel does or does not have a genuine partner for peace. Rather, these security giants demand that Israel once again determine her own destiny.

The Israeli plan, labeled "Security First," assumes a two-state final status arrangement is not currently feasible. It is impossible to eradicate terrorism through force alone. Continuation of the diplomatic impasse will lead to further violence. And Israel is strong enough to offer an independent initiative that combines security, civil, economic, and political measures.

In the security realm, the IDF will remain deployed in the West Bank until a final status arrangement is reached, and the security fence will be completed, enhancing security within the Green Line and for 80 percent of Israelis living in the West Bank.

In the civil-economic realm, the welfare of Palestinians will be improved by establishing an international fund to rehabilitate Palestinian communities and increasing work permits.

Importantly, the Knesset should pass an evacuation compensation law, encouraging settlers now living east of the security fence, outside the security fence, to relocate west of the fence. What an impactful message that would send about Israel intentions.

In the political realm, Israel should accept the Arab Peace Initiative with adjustments to accommodate Israel's security and demographic needs as a basis for negotiations; acknowledge that Palestinian neighborhoods of east Jerusalem will be part of the future Palestinian state; and implement a freeze on settlement expansion east of the security fence, like Dr. Pollock mentioned.

In Gaza, reconciliation with Turkey is an important opportunity to hold the ceasefire, address humanitarian needs, and promote economic development, including a seaport subject to Israeli security and PA control.

Mr. Chairman, why have Israel's most decorated security officials grown frustrated with their own government's lack of initiative? Israel's top military minds have come to understand the inescapable truth that the creation of a demilitarized Palestinian state is not a gift to the Palestinians; rather, it is the only way Israel will remain a Jewish and democratic state.

In conclusion, Mr. Chairman, demographic trends clarify the need for separation. The Jewish population from the Mediterranean Sea to the Jordan River is now 52 percent. In 2020, it will be 49 percent; in 2030, only 44 percent Jewish. Separation into two states, following the Security First plan, is essential for Israel to remain a democratic, Jewish-majority state.

Thank you.

[The prepared statement of Mr. Wexler follows:]

Testimony
The Honorable Robert Wexler
President, S. Daniel Abraham Center for Middle East Peace

House Committee on Foreign Affairs

Financially Rewarding Terrorism in the West Bank

July 6, 2016

Chairman Royce, Ranking Member Engel, Members of the Committee.

Israel is often coined the Start-Up Nation highlighting the Jewish State's economic miracle and technological and scientific achievements. Just as remarkable is another defining characteristic. Against all odds, Israeli military forces have successfully defended against an onslaught of hostile forces since 1948.

For those of us who are Zionists, the unprecedented security collaboration between the United States and Israel is a source of tremendous pride. The joint development of missile defense technologies, all-time high intelligence sharing, historic military training exercises, and the delivery of the F-35 Joint Strike Fighter, all demonstrate the unbreakable bond between us and Israel. American administrations and Congress after Congress have ensured Israel's qualitative military advantage. Israel's defense and intelligence coordination with Egypt and Jordan is unprecedented.

Despite these positive developments, the Middle East Quartet released its report last week asserting that the policies of both Israelis and Palestinians have distanced a two state outcome, creating a dynamic in which a one state reality has taken root. The Quartet calls on the Palestinian Authority to stop incitement of violence, bolster efforts to prevent terrorism and condemn attacks against Israelis. Likewise, the Quartet calls on Israel to cease settlement expansion, transfer civilian authority to the PA in Area C of the West Bank and bluntly questions Israel's long-term intentions.

With this backdrop of despair and lack of trust on both sides, a stunning development has occurred. The most compelling group now advocating for a two state solution is the Israeli security establishment. Two weeks ago, a group of over 200 retired generals or equivalent rank from the Israeli Defense Forces, Mossad, Shin Bet, and Israel Police redirected the political discourse. Boldly, Israel's most patriotic soldiers cast aside the question of whether Israel does or does not have a genuine partner for peace. Rather, these security giants demand that Israel once again determine her own destiny.

The Israeli plan, labeled Security First, assumes: a two-state final status arrangement is not currently feasible; it is impossible to eradicate terrorism through force alone; continuation of the diplomatic impasse will lead to further violence; and Israel is strong enough to offer an independent initiative that combines security, civil-economic, and political measures.

In the security realm, the IDF will remain deployed in the West Bank until a final status arrangement is reached and the security fence will be completed enhancing security within the Green Line and for 80% of Israelis living in the West Bank.

In the civil-economic realm, the welfare of Palestinians will be improved by establishing an international fund to rehabilitate Palestinian communities and increasing work permits. Importantly, the Knesset should pass an 'Evacuation-Compensation Law' encouraging settlers living east of the security fence to relocate west of the fence. What an impactful message that would send about Israeli intentions.

In the political realm, Israel should accept the Arab Peace Initiative, with adjustments to accommodate Israel's security and demographic needs as a basis for negotiations; acknowledge that Palestinian neighborhoods of East Jerusalem will be part of the future Palestinian state, and implement a freeze on settlement expansion east of the security fence.

In Gaza, reconciliation with Turkey is an opportunity to hold the cease fire, address humanitarian needs and promote economic development including a sea port subject to Israeli security and PA control.

Mr. Chairman, why have Israel's most decorated security officials grown frustrated with their own government's lack of initiative? Israel's top military minds have come to understand the inescapable truth—that the creation of a demilitarized Palestinian state is not a gift to the Palestinians. Rather, it is the only way Israel can remain a Jewish and Democratic state.

Demographic trends clarify the need for separation. The Jewish population from the Mediterranean Sea to the Jordan River is now 52%; in 2020, it will be 49% and in 2030, only 44% Jewish. Separation into two states following the Security First plan is essential for Israel to remain a democratic, Jewish majority state.

Thank you.

Chairman ROYCE. Thank you.

We are going to go with a question I have to Mr. Carmon.

The PA has, as you know, long faced a lot of criticism from Western governments for its policy of paying Palestinian prisoners or the families of prisoners in Israeli jails. And we here in Congress have, you know, consistently passed legislation over the last few years that requires restrictions on financial aid to the Palestinian Authority based on the amounts spent on these salaries.

The problem that I want to raise is one, as you note in your testimony, where you say, bowing to international pressure, the PA stopped paying from one PA ministry, only to restart the payment through an arm of the PLO. And this duplicity was not explained to us by our Government at the time that we did some cross-examination on this. Now it is surfacing.

Can you help walk us through that change? When was it made? How hard is it to track? Give us the details on what happened there.

Mr. CARMON. Yes, sir.

In May 2014, under the pressure of donor countries, the PA made a deliberate move of misleading those countries by transferring the distribution of the money that comes from the PA to a body of the PLO.

It created a virtual body, I should say, called the Commission for Detainees and Ex-Detainees Affairs, which belongs to the PLO, but it was virtual in the sense that the offices remained the same offices; the man in charge was the same man, Issa Qaraqe, with a different job title; the supervision or oversight of the distribution of the money remained the same.

And it was all in answer to this pressure which was specified by the minister at the time of the affairs of the prisoners, Mr. Ziad Abu Ein, who said we had to do it because of the pressure of donor countries which began different investigations about how we spend this money.

So this was the idea, we pass it to the PLO. And this is the end of the story. They will not——

Chairman ROYCE. And, as I recall, in terms of the dollar amount, it was precisely the same amount——

Mr. CARMON. Absolutely.

Chairman ROYCE [continuing]. To the dollar that was transferred.

Mr. CARMON. Yep.

Chairman ROYCE. How much of the annual PA budget is taken up by these salaries to terrorists? What percentage?

Mr. CARMON. This is hard to determine because no one knows really what is the PA general budget. Much of it is hidden. There are different bodies that are dealing with it. But I would say that by the——

Chairman ROYCE. Of the known budget.

Mr. CARMON [continuing]. Online and—right. Maybe it would be about 10 percent.

Chairman ROYCE. About 10 percent——

Mr. CARMON. Yes.

Chairman ROYCE [continuing]. Goes to reward people——

Mr. CARMON. Right.

Chairman ROYCE [continuing]. To carry out attacks, stabbings, and shootings of the Israel population.

Mr. CARMON. Mr. Chairman, the President of the Palestinian Authority said openly that this is the main concern of the Palestinians, that the prisoners are a fighting sector of our society and they——

Chairman ROYCE. But most of these prisoners are young people. You know, the targeting goes to children, the targeting goes to youth. They are recruiting young people. I saw one of the recordings the other day of a girl who looked no more than 5. Maybe she was 4. "What message would you send to other children?" And she has a knife in her hand, and she says, "Stab, stab, stab," is the message she sends. That is the kind of programming.

In Congress here, over and over again, we repeat this theme: If you want to make peace, you have to teach peace. This is what we keep conveying to the Palestinian Authority. But what we are watching on their television is exactly the opposite.

Maybe you can comment on this messaging and what it constitutes.

Mr. CARMON. Mr. Chairman, MEMRI has been monitoring the Arab and Palestinian media mindset for almost 20 years, and what we see in the Palestinian media—and now it is virtual, it is online, and it goes all over the world—is a constant legitimatization of the armed action, of the killing of Israelis and Jews. And much of the terminology refers to Jews, kill the Jews.

We have so much material online on our Web site, MEMRI.org, which shows it in a quite graphic way, pictures of the actual killing, reacting and acting in a kindergarten of the terrorist acts, to tell people, this is the model, this is the—tell kids, this is your model.

But there is more than that. There is actual training through the Internet of how to do it.

Chairman ROYCE. On how to do it.

Mr. CARMON. Not just stab as it comes to you, but where to hit. And there are instructions, and there are instructions to use poison, with which knives to deal, and, of course, to use any weapon possible, not necessarily weapons but cars and trucks and other ways, whatever is in your capability—kill, kill, kill.

Chairman ROYCE. And these are official Palestinian Authority media?

Mr. CARMON. Much of it is on the Palestinian official media, absolutely.

Chairman ROYCE. Yeah.

Well, my time has expired. I will go to Mr. Eliot Engel of New York.

Mr. ENGEL. Thank you, Mr. Chairman.

We all know that the Palestinian Authority has not lived up to its promises, and we are talking about their incitement against Israelis and Jews. And we know that the disgusting spectacle of paying terrorists for crimes, for murders, calling them martyrs is something that really, really irks all of us.

But, on the other hand, you know, you look at President Abbas; he has just completed 11 years of his 4-year term. He threatens to quit all the time. I would like to hear anybody's response about if should we worry about a PA collapse. They are no prize package, but breathing down their neck is Hamas.

Is that something that we should be worried about, if the PA just totally collapsed? Could Hamas take over? Would the Israelis have something on their hands, that they really would not want to go in and retake the area? Any thoughts on the matter?

I have no regard for Abbas and what he has done, but what about the potential of the collapse of the PA? Anybody who would care to answer.

Mr. Wexler.

Mr. WEXLER. Mr. Engel raises an important point. President Abbas presents a mixed bag at best. And he is responsible, ultimately, for all of the atrocities that have been outlined this morning. But there is also another aspect, which is that the collaboration between the PA and Israel is, in fact, quite substantial.

Now, Abbas isn't collaborating with the Israel security forces because he has become a Zionist. Just the opposite. He is collaborating because it is in his best interest to do so. Why? Because if he didn't, the more extreme guys, Hamas—and now there are even more extreme guys than Hamas—would threaten the relative stability in the West Bank.

So, to your point, Congressman Engel, if the PA were to collapse, what we are likely to see is not a more democratic regime, unfortunately. The gap is likely to be filled by an even more extreme bunch.

But let's also be fair, if we may. Condemnations of President Abbas are fair, they are legitimate, again, outlined this morning. But everyone here needs to understand what it takes in order to have an election in the Palestinian Authority. You need three approvals. The PA has to approve. Israel has to approve, because you can't hold an election in Jerusalem without Israeli approval. And you have to have Hamas to approve because you can't have votes in Gaza, unfortunately, without them.

So I am not casting judgment, but we need to be realistic about the enormous process that would need to be undertaken in order to actually have an election under the current circumstances in the Palestinian territories. You need those three actors to agree to some type of election administration.

Mr. ENGEL. Thank you.

One of the things that is interesting in terms of the geopolitical movement of the Middle East is that, if you talk to heads of state, the Sunni Arab states sound very similar in their perspective of the Middle East to the Israeli leadership, to Netanyahu. And you will talk about Iran and other things, and you talk to the Sunni Arab states; it is the same thing.

When you speak with Israeli leadership, they will say there is no conflict with the Arab world. There is a conflict with the Palestinians. But the Arab world, the Sunni world, sees the situation today much like the Israeli Government. There is unprecedented cooperation going on behind the scenes between Israel and some of the countries that were long regarded as Israel's enemies.

So it is interesting, when you look at the Arab League putting forth a comprehensive proposal and a peace plan. There have been media reports recently that Prime Minister Netanyahu is open to discussing the Arab Peace Initiative as the basis for an accord. Israel rightly takes issue with several parts of the proposal, but that could potentially be worked out.

To what extent should the U.S. encourage this? Anybody else?

Mr. Pollock?

Mr. POLLOCK. Thank you very much for the question and the opportunity to reflect on it.

I believe that the Arab Peace Initiative is a significant step forward, although, as you and others have pointed out, it doesn't implement itself, and it needs to be negotiated, and it needs to be revised.

But I would point out that U.S. support for discussions about the Arab Peace Initiative could be an important new ingredient in this picture going forward.

Secretary Kerry achieved an important modification of the Arab Peace Initiative a few years ago when the Arab foreign ministers formally agreed that Israel's withdrawal from occupied territories could be, on the basis of new boundaries, negotiated between the parties that would allow for territorial exchanges—land swaps, as they are often called—rather than literally on the pre-1967 lines.

But that achievement, unfortunately, in the last couple of years, has been taken back, walked back by Arab governments and by the Arab League. It would be useful, I think, for the United States to go to them, to the Arab governments, and say: You agreed to this a few years ago. Can we assume that you still agree to it today? Can we proceed on that basis?

That would allow for negotiations that would advance this emerging consensus between Israel and key Arab governments that peace is in their common interest.

One last point about this. In late 2013, Arab foreign ministers were prepared to go even further, at the urging of Secretary Kerry, but they were stopped by objections from the Palestinian Authority. This is not in the public record, but it is a fact.

The Palestinian Authority objected, successfully and very sadly, in my view, to a willingness on the part of other Arab leaders to accept the formulation of recognition of Israel as a Jewish state or as a state for the Jewish people. And it would be useful today for the United States to encourage those Arab governments to reconsider and to encourage the Palestinian Authority, hard as it would be—and it would be very hard—to reconsider its objections to that formulation. That could be a new and, I think, very hopeful basis for renewed peace negotiations.

Thank you.

Mr. ENGEL. Thank you, Mr. Chairman.

Chairman ROYCE. Mr. Rohrabacher.

Mr. ROHRABACHER. Thank you very much.

And, first of all, I would like to thank the chairman, Mr. Royce, for conducting this hearing.

And I would sign on personally to your concept that, if money is going to people who have committed acts of terrorism by the Palestinian Authority, that that should be extracted from our commitment to aid the Palestinian Authority. So I think that is a very good step, symbolic as well, but needs to be done.

I would also like to especially identify myself with the remarks of Ranking Member Engel. His commitment—and as we have heard from the witnesses, as well—for a two-state solution has not been dimmed by some of the horrendous downsides and setbacks that we have seen in the last 20 years.

And this two-state solution was a solution that was worked out. There was a great deal of optimism that it could work. Let me just suggest—I just got back from the Middle East, and I was in Egypt, Jordan, and Turkey. And the average people in those countries still believe in the two-state solution—the average people. They are not pro-Israeli, but they understand that, to have peace, they need this two-state solution. That was heartening to me.

What is disheartening to me is that we have the United States still acting so foolishly that we end up providing hundreds of millions of dollars to people who then spend tens of millions, if not more, building the very tunnels that Ranking Member Engel mentioned.

And I remember walking with you down into those tunnels. And, by the way, these tunnels are not just little holes in the ground. These are engineering efforts that are very expensive, engineering projects that I am sure cost tens of millions of dollars. And yet we continue, to make this consistent with what the chairman is saying, we continue to finance them at the same level.

I would suggest we make a list and that, when the Palestinians are obviously using their resources to conduct war on Israel, we should extract that from what we are giving to the Palestinian Authority and et cetera.

So, with that said—and, also, it is always great to hear former Congressman Wexler. He is almost as passionate as I am about things, and that is saying a lot.

Just one question for Mr. Pollock.

You said that perhaps it would be good for Israel to cease its tactic of tearing down buildings. It is my understanding that the Israelis destroy buildings when someone in the family who lived in that building has conducted a terrorist attack and murdered some kind of an Israeli citizen.

Don't you think that unilaterally ceasing that policy would not be something that would give them encouragement to stop the type of terrorism that this hearing is all about?

Mr. POLLOCK. Thank you, sir. That is a fair question.

The reality, as I understand it, actually is that, yes, that is current policy of the Israeli Government. Although they had stopped doing that for many years, they resumed it in the last couple of years in response to the new wave of stabbings and other killings.

But the truth is that the Israeli Government demolishes many, many other Palestinian buildings for various other reasons—just, for example, not having proper building permits, not allowing Palestinian construction in certain areas of the West Bank or of East Jerusalem and so on.

And I believe, applied that way, this is a counterproductive tactic.

Mr. ROHRABACHER. Well, as long as that caveat was put on, in terms of we will continue our destruction of those buildings that have a direct association with people who have committed acts of terrorism, well, then I might agree with that.

Mr. POLLOCK. Yes, sir.

Mr. ROHRABACHER. And one note. The Palestinians lost their land in 1948, all right? We understand that. And the Israelis that started their new country in 1948, they are a nation now. And I agree with Mr. Wexler's analysis that, for it to be the Israel that is a separate country and will have some hope, that it has to be recognized as a Jewish state and the right of return.

As long as that is a demand and that has not—people keep ignoring that issue. As long as that has not been accepted, that Palestinian refugees from 1948 are not going to be able to go back into what is now the state of Israel, there will be no peace, because there is no—Israel would never accept that because it would be the end of their country.

So I would hope that the Palestinian people decide that they do want to live at peace and accept that there is no right of return and that there is a two-state solution. So let us be optimistic that that someday can be achieved, while understanding that today this terrorism that motivated the chairman to call this hearing, that that is dealt with.

So thank you very much to the witnesses.

Chairman ROYCE. Thank you.

We go to Mr. Albio Sires of New Jersey.

Mr. SIRES. Thank you, Mr. Chairman.

Thank you for being here today.

Congressman Wexler, nice to see you. I see the passion is still there, which is great.

You know, I keep thinking about this money that is paid out. I cannot imagine that the donor countries who are trying to help make these payments cannot help, cannot be—what is the word I want here? What I am trying to say is, will the will be in those countries to stop payment? Is there a will to do that? Or will they just keep running along with the program? Can anybody answer that?

I mean, I would think it would be very easy, if the will was there, to say, well, we are not going to give you any money if you are going to pay for these people who—the families of people who commit atrocities. Why isn't the will there to stop that? It seems to me, anyway. Maybe I am wrong.

Mr. CARMON. Well, it is hard to know what are the motives of the donor countries. They begin pressuring, and they hope that this pressure will help, but, instead of a real change, they got a virtual change.

And, really, the point to raise, as I mentioned, is that Abbas himself is doing it for the wrong reasons, so why wouldn't they? It is not something that is undone. It is something possible, and Abbas himself is doing it.

Mr. SIRES. But I am talking about European countries giving money, and people are committing atrocities. They get the money, Abbas gets the money and doles it out. But I think it should come from the people who give the money to Abbas who have the will and say, hey, we are not going to give you a dime if you keep using the money for this.

I mean, there is no will there. And then yet, you know, they are the first ones who criticize Israel all the time.

Mr. CARMON. Sir, it is also U.S. money.

Mr. SIRES. Well, that——

Mr. WEXLER. If I may, directly to the point, but also to the broader, I think, aim of this committee and to each and every member of the committee, which is ultimately assist the parties to create a dynamic in which a two-state outcome is feasible—a homeland for the Palestinian state and a demilitarized Palestinian state, and a Jewish homeland in a democratic Israel.

Now, rightfully, the chairman and this committee is focused on terrorism and payments and the like. But I can tell you, this document that was prepared by 200-plus Israeli generals, these guys are not doves. And what they will say first is, yes, go after incitement, yes, go after terrorism, yes, do all the things that you are talking about today, but you are still not going to resolve or even begin to resolve the problem.

And to resolve this problem, it is going to have to be multifaceted, and it is going to have to address the incitements on all side. And I am not creating a relativity between terrorism and building houses. I am not doing that. There is no relativity about terrorism. But we also need to understand that, from a Palestinian perspective, Israel occupies the West Bank. And I don't say the term ''occupation'' in the politically loaded way. They control it. But when that control is exerted, oftentimes for very legitimate reasons, there are counter-reactions.

And we need to understand that if we want to help the parties we need to address all aspects of that conflict—economic, political, and also people to people, much of what has been discussed. Should security be first? Yes, of course it should. Should terrorism and payments to terrorists be completely not tolerated? Of course. But just to address that, we shouldn't be so unrealistic or naive to think that terrorism is going to be somehow mitigated.

Mr. SIRES. We have to start somewhere.

Dr. Pollock?

Mr. POLLOCK. Yes, thanks.

I think that this should not be viewed as an all-or-nothing proposition in the sense that we either have to cut off the PA completely or do nothing. I think that there——

Mr. SIRES. I am more concerned about the European countries.

Mr. POLLOCK. Okay.

Mr. SIRES. Because we put stipulations in the money that we give.

Mr. POLLOCK. Well, yes, but the U.S. stipulations, as my fellow witness here, Mr. Carmon, has observed, have been evaded by the PA through this deceitful technique of funneling money to terrorists and their families under a different name, right?

So I think that the United States could and other countries should—although we can't control what they do in Europe or other places—should reduce the amount or condition the amount of assistance that they provide to the PA without threatening to or without actually cutting it off completely. Because there is a real danger, as someone else pointed out, of the PA collapsing, which would be bad for everyone—Palestinians, Israelis, Americans, and the region as a whole.

But I do think that a certain calibrated, limited amount of financial pressure applied, again, by the United States without any loopholes or escape hatches and, if possible, by European and other donors to the PA would be helpful in addressing this immediate issue. And I agree strongly with Mr. Wexler that this not the only issue on the table, but we do have to start somewhere.

I want to say one other last point in this regard. I think it is quite possible in the real world, unfortunately, that if we and/or European donors reduce—not cut off, but reduce—the amount of assistance to the PA by the amount, say, with which they subsidize terrorists and their families, if we do that, it is quite possible that other unfriendly governments or not-so-friendly governments would jump in to fill the gap—Arab governments, perhaps others.

And that may be—I hate to say it, to be so cynical about it, but that may be the only way in which any of those governments will fulfill their aid pledges to the Palestinians.

Mr. SIRES. Yeah. I do not think that one issue is going to solve everything. It is much more complex than that.

Chairman ROYCE. Joe Wilson of South Carolina.

Mr. WILSON. Thank you, Chairman.

And I appreciate so much Chairman Ed Royce, Ranking Member Eliot Engel. This is an extraordinary example of bipartisan concern and capable people. And I am grateful to be here with my colleague Albio Sires, too, and ask questions which really are quite in line.

It is just absolutely appalling to me that we have a situation with the Palestinian Authority which is providing rewards to murderers' families. It is pay to slay. And every effort, I think, should be made to stop it. Sadly, this follows the dangerous Iranian nuclear deal, where funding is being provided by the Iranians to Hamas.

And we need to remember that just last week there was another rocket attack at Sderot. And I personally identify with that. I have been to Sderot. I have met a dear lady who was at a park with her children when a rocket attack occurred. She grabbed the closest child, went to a shelter. But the child that she didn't pick up was permanently traumatized. I never want to see American families have to face this.

But the thought that we would be allowing any type of financing for pay to slay or for Hamas and its—by releasing funds to Iran, putting American and Israeli families at risk.

Along with this, the Palestinian Authority is providing financial support for pay to slay, for terrorism in the region.

And, Dr. Pollock, the—and it has been reviewed, but the American people need to know again, so restate. How does the Palestinian Authority provide support of the families of known terrorists? Is it in the form of cash, electronic wire transfers, other sources of payment? And what is the total amount that the Palestinian Authority provides in compensation to these families each year? Is there any evidence that U.S. dollars are ultimately ending up in the pockets of the relatives of terrorists?

And you have stated it, but state it one more time.

Mr. CARMON. Sir, the documents are there. The information is there. We also possess much of it online. I have in my hand documents from the Arab Bank and from the Ministry of Detainees, which sets up all the details, everything that—how and where.

And they are respectable banks. It is an official government operation. It is not some rogue side payment under the table. This is what the PA stands for, ideologically and in money.

So the information is there. It is, again, the will to act upon it. And I think that it would be a great educational process if that amount of $300 million per year is cut so people understand through their lives that this path is not the way to get rid neither of the occupation nor of their life conditions.

Mr. WILSON. And thank you again for restating and holding up the records. And if that wasn't clear, of course, the propaganda that you have cited, too, and the boasting about the murder of the young lady last week, the teenager, stabbing to death, is just incredible.

Congressman Wexler, welcome back. In your opinion, what is the impact of the Palestinian Authority's financial support to the families of terrorists on future acts of terrorism? Do you believe these payments encourage and perpetuate further acts of violence?

Mr. WEXLER. Of course they do. How could they not?

And not only are they destructive, as everyone has described, in terms of the implications for individuals, but they are also destructive in terms of its implication for the two societies. Why should the Israelis ever believe that they have a genuine partner for peace when the other side is encouraging the type of behavior that is being discussed? And, likewise, if you are a 12-, 13-, 14-year-old young Palestinian boy and you see the type of behavior that is encouraged on your side, what disincentive is there to go and repeat those kinds of atrocities?

But, if I may, and not, again, to create any relative type of comparison, but that is why those of us who care so deeply about the security and the well-being of Israel need to make certain that Israel takes independent initiatives on its own behalf to control its own destiny, quite frankly, not wait for the partner to emerge that we all hope would emerge.

And that is the kind of behavior that, ultimately, as it stands, will actually create a dynamic that might possibly, if the Palestinian leadership wants to become more reasonable, will be able to do so.

Mr. WILSON. Well, thank you very much. And, again, I look forward to working with my colleagues to ending pay for slay. Thank you.

Chairman ROYCE. Thank you.

We go to Karen Bass from California.

Ms. BASS. Thank you very much, Mr. Chair.

First of all, you know, my heart goes out to the family of the 13-year-old child. I can't imagine what they must be going through right now. But, yeah, I am so concerned about the cycle of violence, and I hope that this atrocity doesn't lead to revenge killings like we have seen.

38

And I think both Mr. Wexler and Dr. Pollock have talked about the generals and the desire of the generals to see a different policy. And I wanted to know if you could expand on that a little bit.

A couple of my colleagues have mentioned—and I believe you did too, Dr. Pollock—about the policy of destroying homes—and I would imagine the home of the 17-year-old might get destroyed— and then the policy of the PA of giving money to families that have committed these acts.

So when a house is blown up, then where does that family go? And is that an example of the money that the PA uses? I mean, what happens to—you never hear about that. And you also mentioned other examples of houses being, you know, dismantled because of building codes or whatever. What happens to those families?

Mr. POLLOCK. Okay. Thank you for the question.

In my own view, blowing up the houses of families of terrorists, if that actually deters terrorism——

Ms. BASS. Is there any evidence of this?

Mr. POLLOCK [continuing]. I don't know the answer to that, honestly. But if—if—it does deter terrorism, then I think, tragically, it would be acceptable, even though, honestly, it is collective punishment. It leaves families who may not actually be responsible for the actions of their children or other relatives, it leaves them homeless.

It is something that is very debatable. And, as I said, the Israeli Government itself had long stopped using that practice and only resumed it in recent years, I would say, almost as a matter of desperation, because they were subject to this very deadly wave of stabbings and other forms of assault.

Ms. BASS. Is this a practice that the 200 generals are against?

Mr. POLLOCK. I don't know for sure, but——

Mr. WEXLER. No, I—oh, I am sorry.

Mr. POLLOCK [continuing]. I want to just say in connection with that—and allow me to be very frank. With all due respect to any group of generals or others who are well-intentioned and smart and patriotic, here or anywhere, it is the Government of Israel that has to make these decisions. And that government is, like it or not, a democratically elected government. And only a democratic election will change that government or its policies.

Ms. BASS. I believe both of you have made reference to settlements and saying that more settlements shouldn't be approved. But weren't more settlements just approved in the last couple days?

Mr. WEXLER. If I may?

Obviously, I don't speak for Dr. Pollock, but, actually, I think we have been talking on the same tune. What we have talked about is the security fence that Israel, in my humble opinion, rightfully built after the last round of intifada. And, unfortunately, for political reasons, they haven't completed the fence, but that is a whole other story.

What Dr. Pollock and I have said is, beyond that security fence, meaning east of the security fence—and the route of the security fence was created by the Israeli Government—that the Israelis should stop building beyond that fence. Because, for all practical purposes, based on an Israeli action, the likelihood that that land would ever become a part of an Israeli state in a negotiated outcome is probably zero percent. So why exacerbate—why create even additional problems?

Dr. Pollock, I think, talked about a tradeoff. What he said was, in return for the Israeli Government saying they would not and, in fact, not building beyond the fence—he talked about a tradeoff—then America shouldn't criticize settlement building within the fence. And I think that is a legitimate point.

But settlements don't occur in a vacuum, or building doesn't occur in a vacuum. You have to put all the issues before the people. But if you did that kind of action, if the Israelis did that kind of action, their international legitimacy for those that are at least objective would go sky-high. Because you wouldn't be able to just criticize the Israeli Government in a wholehearted way without recognizing the fact that they have taken an important initial step.

Ms. BASS. Thank you.

Chairman ROYCE. We go to Jeff Duncan of South Carolina.

Mr. DUNCAN. Thank you, Mr. Chairman, and thanks for this hearing.

When I think about the issues of today, I think about the solution. And I think the solution is easy, but the political implementation of that solution seems very, very difficult. When I say "solution," I mean the beginning of a solution. And that is the recognition by the PA, the Palestinians, of the Jewish state of Israel's right to exist—recognition of that state.

When I was in Israel in 2011, I talked with Benjamin Netanyahu and Shimon Peres and others, who said, you know, if the Palestinians would just recognize our right to exist, it would go a long way to getting us all to table to start negotiating the things that the gentlemen on the panel are talking about.

The solution is easy, but the political implementation by the Palestinians is very difficult, and I get that. I get that. But sometimes leadership takes making difficult decisions to move the ball forward. So my appeal to the Palestinians today is recognize Israel.

I am proud to stand as a Member of Congress as someone that stands with the state of Israel and support them in any way that I can as a Congressman and we as the Foreign Affairs Committee and the United States Congress can—financially, security-wise, and just verbally of standing firm in our commitment to the state of Israel.

Mr. Chairman, this hearing is important, but it is difficult for me today to focus on Israel and the West Bank and the U.N. and recognition and funding after I witnessed yesterday in my own country the FBI Director erode the very fabric of the fabric of the foundations of the institutions of government.

July 5, 2016, will be a day that we remember, when we saw that the blindfold on the arbiter of the scales of justice was ripped away. Because the scales of justice are no longer blindfolded. Before yesterday, you were to be judged and weighted based on the evidence. But as of yesterday, political influence, party affiliation, race, gender, family ties, you name it, all will factor into justice.

American needs to realize that the scales of justice wear a blindfold for a reason. It is what sets us apart from other countries around the world. I travel extensively through Latin America as chairman of the Western Hemisphere Subcommittee. What sets America apart from countries in Latin America is our impartial justice system, where the facts are weighed.

It shouldn't matter what family you were born into, your wealth, your race, your sex. It shouldn't. And we have had an ongoing conversation in the last few years about race and impartiality with regard to race in the justice system. Now we are going to have an ongoing conversation about political aristocracy, political connections, wealth, future aspirations, you name it—will all factor into the American judicial system to its detriment, America.

Regardless of how you feel about individuals and individual candidates, surely you believe in the institutions of government.

It is a sad day for me. I can't focus on Israel and the topics that the gentlemen on the panel were brought to Washington to discuss. My love for Israel is clouded by my love for the United States of America. Because without America, without the things that we believe in, we will not have the ability to support our allies in the region. And I hope everyone will think about that.

And, with that, I yield back.

Chairman ROYCE. We go to Mr. Gerry Connolly of Virginia.

Mr. CONNOLLY. Thank you, Mr. Chairman.

Dr. Pollock, I am picking up on your last comment about a democratic government in Israel, and until and unless that democratic government is changed, they make the decisions.

Surely, however, you did not mean to suggest that this democratic elected government, as the largest supporter of Israel, doesn't have a right to be critical when it thinks its interests or even Israel's are at risk.

Mr. POLLOCK. Absolutely not. You are quite right, sir.

Mr. CONNOLLY. Okay.

Mr. POLLOCK. But——

Mr. CONNOLLY. I just wanted to clarify that. I don't mean to cut you off, but I—because leaving it that way—I mean, we get to be, as friends, critical.

Mr. POLLOCK. Yes, sir.

Mr. CONNOLLY. And U.S. policy is longstanding with respect to settlement expansion and other aspects of the relationship that have critical aspects to them as well as, of course, longstanding support. I count myself, certainly, as an unswerving supporter of Israel, but that doesn't mean I can't be critical as a friend.

Mr. POLLOCK. Of course.

Mr. CONNOLLY. Okay.

And you can answer this, too, if you wish, but I will put it to, first, Congressman Wexler.

Congressman Wexler, okay, so there are problems with the Palestinians—leadership, funneling of money, as Dr. Pollock indicated, that, clearly, we find abhorrent.

What happens—let's defund the PA, let's close their offices here, let's stop working with them. Would that be welcomed by the Israeli Government, in your opinion? And would it help the cause, the peace cause?

Mr. WEXLER. It is not my opinion; it is the policy of the Israel Government at successive stages where they were diametrically opposed to certain steps that might have led to a destructive position for the PA.

No one has a greater stake in the success of the Palestinian Authority and, more importantly, a greater stake in the bolstering of moderate forces or, at least, of the group, the most moderate forces, than Israel. If the Palestinian Authority crashes, one of two things is most likely to happen: Hamas or even more extreme elements take control, or the Israelis have to step in even with greater strength. Either result is a disaster for Israel.

Mr. CONNOLLY. And that is the position of the Israeli Government.

Mr. WEXLER. Sure. It has been that way through Labor governments, Likud governments, Kadima governments, because it is, quite frankly, so obvious. They need the Palestinian moderate forces to be successful.

Now, some could argue, when they had that opportunity under Prime Minister Fayyad, who was, you know, in most respects, from an American and Israeli perspective, the best thing that came along——

Mr. CONNOLLY. A vary able administrator.

Mr. WEXLER. That is right.

Mr. CONNOLLY. And, as far as we know, incorruptible.

Mr. WEXLER. Yes. And we didn't do enough, none of us, to push his agenda——

Mr. CONNOLLY. Yeah.

Mr. WEXLER [continuing]. Quite frankly.

Mr. CONNOLLY. Terrible loss, actually, when we lost him.

Dr. Pollock, do you concur?

Mr. POLLOCK. Yes, I do. But, as I said, I don't believe that this is an all-or-nothing——

Mr. CONNOLLY. Right.

Mr. POLLOCK [continuing]. Proposition.

Mr. CONNOLLY. Got it. I agree. I think our choices aren't great, and I think that is always hard for Americans. There ought to be a very clear white-hatted choice and a——

Mr. POLLOCK. Right.

Mr. CONNOLLY [continuing]. Bad, black-hatted choice. We are between a rock and a hard place, but, absent the PA, probably either the Israelis have to step in and actually run everything in the West Bank administratively, in terms of local government services, or Hamas gains control of the West Bank, which is not a desirable outcome.

Mr. POLLOCK. What I mean specifically is that a reduction—not a cutoff, a reduction——

Mr. CONNOLLY. Yeah.

Mr. POLLOCK [continuing]. In U.S. and other funding for the PA——

Mr. CONNOLLY. Right. I didn't mean to even suggest you were saying that. But they have been calls here, even on this committee, for a total cutoff and close the——

Mr. POLLOCK. No. I think that would be a mistake.

Mr. CONNOLLY. Okay.

A final thing, real quickly. Mr. Wexler, you made reference to 200 generals, Mossad leaders, Shin Bet leaders, who have expressed deep concern about the current government in Israel, Netanyahu, and Israel's security. Do you want to elaborate a little bit on that? What is going on?

Mr. WEXLER. Yeah. I don't want to politicize this needlessly. Their concern is not addressed about the government. Their concern is about the policy. Their concern—these are generals. For the most part, almost all of them are not politicians. And what they have put forth is a multifaceted set of policies that will help address the security quagmire that Israel finds itself in.

The first assumption they make, quite frankly, is that the question of whether or not there is a genuine partner for peace for Israel, they don't care about it. Not because they don't want there to be a genuine partner. What they are saying is, if we wait forever for Abbas or his successors to do the right thing, in the meantime we are going to be compromised; our interests, Israeli interests, are going to be compromised.

So what they are saying to their own government, to their own people is: These are the 12, 18 steps we could take on our own, because, thank goodness, we are strong enough, and will enhance our position rather than detract from it. That is what they are saying.

It is not a condemnation or an applause for the government. What they are saying is the status quo, the way it remains, if we do nothing, we will actually compromise Israel's Jewishness, its Jewish majority; its democratic nature is in question, and its international standing is constantly badgered.

Now, for a lot of reasons, that badgering and that criticism is totally illegitimate. But what these security commanders are saying is, if we are going to be strategic, let's at least put forth an international position that allows us to enhance our international relationships, as opposed to constantly being on the defensive.

Chairman ROYCE. We are going to go to Randy Weber of Texas.

Mr. WEBER. Thank you, Mr. Chairman.

Dr. Pollock, I have to say, this is the first hearing I have been at where the first witness said, as I see it, our primary task here is not to debate the underlying issues of the Israeli-Palestinian conflict or U.S. policy in that regard. I thought the hearing was over, at that point. That is an interesting thought.

And then you go on and you say—and that is exactly what we have been doing, by the way, in my opinion. We are debating those underlying issues and how we got here and how those need to change.

Then you go on and you lay out five proposals. And your fifth and final proposal is that the U.S. should publicly support and very vocally encourage others to endorse what we call mutual imbalance—I thought that was a news station, i didn't know; or that is "fair and balanced," isn't it?—but, if necessary, unilateral steps toward peaceful coexistence.

And then you talk about the Israelis stopping the destruction of— destroying buildings of those who perpetrate such violence on innocent men, women, and children.

And you don't say in your comments—and I followed you fairly closely—you don't say in your comments anything about there being unilateral action, perhaps, on the Palestinian side.

And so is it totally out of—I mean, is it just totally out in left field and unrealistic to say, how about some unilateral action on their side? They stop indoctrinating their children—I will give you four examples. Then I will give you a chance to respond.

Stop indoctrinating their children with the message of hate. Quit calling the Jewish people dogs and apes and animals and then trying to kill them as such. Kick out Hamas. Recognize Israel's right to exist, number three. And, fourth and finally, stop funding the terrorism and those that are in jail.

Is there no call for the Palestinians to have any unilateral responsibility, Dr. Pollock?

Mr. POLLOCK. Thank you for the question.

I actually think that I made that call, both in my written statement and in my remarks. I said specifically in my remarks—perhaps you weren't here in the room—that the PA should stop referring to murderers——

Mr. WEBER. Well, I am reading your fifth——

Mr. POLLOCK [continuing]. As martyrs.

Mr. WEBER [continuing]. Point basically says that about Israel. It doesn't say it in this context. So if I missed it, I apologize.

Mr. POLLOCK. I think you did miss it, sir, yes. And I accept your apology.

But what I would like to say in response is that, if you look at my written statement, you will see a long list of unilateral moves that Israel could take and that the Palestinians could and should take, including not referring to murderers as martyrs and recognizing Israel as a Jewish state.

Mr. WEBER. Okay. Fair enough.

Do you agree with that, Mr. Wexler, that the Palestinians should be called upon initially to stop the violence from their end?

Mr. WEXLER. Yeah, 100 percent. You had me totally, Congressman Weber, until you said kick out Hamas. I agreed with every word you said. That may trouble you, but I agreed with every word you said.

Mr. WEBER. Your agreeing with me or the not agreeing with kick out Hamas?

Mr. WEXLER. No, I am all——

Mr. WEBER. That is the part that troubles me.

Mr. WEXLER. I am all for kicking out Hamas, but we need to understand the reality. The reality is the PA doesn't have an army. The reality is the strongest army in the region, thank goodness, is the Israeli Army. They haven't been able to kick out Hamas, unfortunately.

So when we say kick out Hamas and you say the PA should doing that, with what weapons? They don't have them. Now, I don't want to give them the kind of weapons that would be required to kick out Hamas.

But what we also respectfully need to understand, as much as you disdain Hamas, hate Hamas, as much as I disdain them and hate them, as much as the Israelis disdain them and hate them, Abbas hates them even more than you and me.

Mr. WEBER. So this is the lesser of two evils? Is that like the bumper sticker that says, ''Have you hugged your terrorist today?''

Mr. WEXLER. No.

Mr. WEBER. I mean——

Mr. WEXLER. No. No. I wouldn't go that far. Hamas is a despicable terrorist organization that is designed to destroy the state of Israel. If I could stamp them out tomorrow, if I had the power to do it, I would do it.

Mr. WEBER. So if it is not destroying the buildings whereby the perpetrators live in and people get to understand—if you want the force and you don't have the military weapons, you have to have the public understand, number one, you don't teach hatred; number two, those who perpetrate such acts of violence will be dealt with immediately and in a very decisive fashion. Is that wrong?

Mr. WEXLER. No. You are right. But here is the problem. Every 2 years—I used to do it too—we would run commercials and send out leaflets. I imagine in November you will send out—in October, you will send out a whole bunch of stuff, what Congressman Weber has achieved these last 2 years.

So if you are a Palestinian and you are taking a look as to, well, which brand of leadership am I in favor of—Abbas' leadership? He talks about negotiating or—even though he doesn't do it—he talks about a peaceful resistance. And the Palestinian people look at it, even if they are inclined to believe, and they say, what has that bought me for the last 30 years? They don't like it. Whether they are right or wrong, I don't know, but they don't like it.

They look at Hamas and their absolutely atrocious behavior— guess who causes the Israeli Government to make a prisoner swap where they give up thousands for two? Hamas, not the Palestinian Authority. So, unfortunately, what the Palestinian Authority see is they see that this terrorist group, in certain ways, from their completely distorted, horrific logic, is more effective in representing their interests than the more moderate Palestinian leadership.

What we have to do, respectfully, is encourage our friends— Israelis, Arabs, everybody, and Palestinians—to support and bolster the moderate strain so that they have a commercial to run.

Chairman ROYCE. We will go to——

Mr. WEBER. Mr. Chairman, I am going to yield back.

Chairman ROYCE. We will go to Lois Frankel of Florida.

Ms. FRANKEL. Thank you, Mr. Chair. Thank you for this hearing.

And one of the things I have always been grateful, in terms of this Congress, which is often at each other's throats on both sides, is the bipartisan spirit and support of Israel and peace for both Israel and the Palestinians, which is what we are here to talk about today.

You know, I wasn't going to raise this, but one of my colleagues made such a dramatic statement about his disappointment about something that happened yesterday. I agree, in this regard. There was something that happened yesterday that really appalled me, but it is not the same thing that appalled him. One of our Presidential candidates—you can just fill in the blank—praised the late Iraq dictator, Saddam Hussein. He said, "You know what he did well? He killed terrorists. They didn't read them their rights. They didn't talk. If they were a terrorist, it was over."

Now, as I recall—and, Mr. Chair, I would ask unanimous consent to have this article put into the record.

I want to just read from an article dated April 3, 2002, CBS News. It says,

> "Iraq President Saddam Hussein has raised the amount offered to the relatives of suicide bombers from $10,000 per family to $25,000, U.S. Defense Secretary Donald Rumsfeld said Wednesday. Since Iraq upped its payments last month, 12 suicide bombers have successfully struck inside Israel, including one man who killed 25 Israelis, many of them elderly, as they sat down to a meal at a hotel to celebrate the Jewish holiday of Passover. The families of three suicide bombers said they recently received payments of $25,000."

So, just for the record, yes, something that I think was disgraceful to American values was any Presidential candidate who would praise Saddam Hussein.

Now, with that said, I am going to ask a question, not on that subject.

Mr. Wexler, I have been very long interested in your analysis of the demographics in the region. And I am told that you did talk about that earlier in your testimony. So my question to you is—and maybe you can just repeat some of that for me—is, what is the incentive for the Palestinians really to not just wait?

Mr. WEXLER. Thank you, Congresswoman Frankel.

This is part of the problem. Time is arguably on the Palestinian side, not on the Israeli side.

If you boil this conflict down—and I don't mean to be simplistic, but—there are three major components, essentially, at least from an Israeli perspective: Land, democracy, and Jewish majority.

The unfortunate reality is Israel gets to pick two of those three. They don't get to pick three. If they take all the land from the Mediterranean to the Jordan River, if they take a great bulk of the West Bank, they are going to either lose their Jewish majority or their democratic nature, which for most of us would be tragic.

So Israel has to choose between two of those three categories. And what the commanders are choosing, what I hope our allies would help create a dynamic in which Israel feels secure enough, strong enough to choose, is a resolution in which their Jewish nature is assured, their democratic nature is assured, and that they get international borders finally.

Israel does not have internationally recognized borders. They need internationally recognized borders that are, in fact, defensible. And that is what the Israeli security establishment is so concerned about. They want to get about the job of protecting Israel. But today that job is so much more difficult because Israel doesn't have internationally recognized borders. And the key component is to create them so that Israel can maintain its Jewish majority and its democratic nature.

Ms. FRANKEL. Thank you.

Chairman ROYCE. We go now to Scott Perry of Pennsylvania.

Mr. PERRY. Thank you, Mr. Chairman.

I would like to drag this hearing back to what I thought it was about, which is financially rewarding terrorism in the West Bank and with an eye toward that.

The U.S. policy toward the Palestinians consists of three end goals: To establish a stable—I am just reading them—lasting and peaceful end to the Israeli-Palestinian conflict through direct bilateral negotiations, that is one; two, to counter Palestinian terrorist groups; and, three, to establish norms of democracy, accountability, and good governance.

Now, the U.S. funding of the United Nations Relief and Works Agency for Palestinian Refugees in the Near East, or UNRWA, as we usually call it, runs counter to every single one of these three policy goals. UNRWA's ties to what I characterize and what many of us characterize as a terrorist organization, Hamas, both threaten bilateral negotiations and undermine U.S. efforts to counter Palestinian terrorist groups.

Since 2006, Hamas-affiliated candidates have held all 11 seats on the UNRWA teachers' union executive board. UNRWA schools use textbooks and materials that delegitimize Israel, denigrate Jews, and venerate martyrdom. These materials work to indoctrinate the Palestinian youth, making them susceptible to radical militant groups such as Hamas.

The unfortunate yet foreseeable result of this curriculum can be seen in an April 2016 poll that found that 78.6 percent of the youth in Gaza and 46.4 percent of the youth in the West Bank support the Knife Intifada. Furthermore, 76 percent of the terrorists taking part in the Knife Intifada were under the age of 30. Now, UNRWA's education system seems to have created a large pool of indoctrinated youth hellbent on attacking Israelis.

UNRWA's employees are screened for ties to terrorism, but the vetting system, believe it or not, focuses on things like al-Qaeda or the Taliban but does not focus on Hamas or Hezbollah. It is crazy. Ninety-five-point-five percent of Palestinians in the West Bank and Gaza believe the Palestinian Authority is corrupt, and 82 percent of Gazans believe Hamas is corrupt. Yet UNRWA effectively works as a support service for both of these organizations, taking care of basic government services. This, in effect, subsidizes with American dollars these groups' corrupt and oftentimes terroristic activities.

The total annual budget for the United Nations Relief and Works Agency for Palestinian Refugees in the Near East, or UNRWA, for Fiscal Year 2015 was $1,246,802,614. And since its inception in 1950, the United States has contributed more than $5.6 billion to the agency, more than any other single nation. And in Fiscal Year 2015, the United States contributed $390.5 million, making up 31 percent of the agency's budget.

Do any of you fine gentlemen on the panel object to my legislation, which would prevent U.S. taxpayers from continuing to fund this agency?

Mr. WEXLER. I don't know if I object or I support it. I certainly support the intention. But, if I may, let's say you pass your legislation, let's say it is implemented and UNRWA and Gaza closes up—

——

Mr. PERRY. It doesn't close up; we just don't fund it anymore.

Mr. WEXLER. Well——

Mr. PERRY. My tax dollars, your tax dollars, their tax dollars don't fund it anymore.

Mr. WEXLER. I get it. And we pay a disproportionate amount of UNRWA dollars based on the U.N. formula. So when your legislation is successful and UNRWA no longer can implement the programs it implements in Gaza, the ones you are objecting to, rightfully so, who is going to run the sewer plant, the one that is already pushing sewage into the sea that not only destroys the Palestinian coast but the Israeli coast? What are those children going to do——

Mr. PERRY. I guess somebody is going to have to make a decision on what their priorities are.

Mr. WEXLER. Okay. All right. All right.

Mr. PERRY. I say that a dirty sea and sewage is bad, but it is better than people being stabbed, blown up, rocketed, et cetera.

Mr. WEXLER. Totally agree with you.

Mr. PERRY. Okay.

Mr. WEXLER. But let's also be realistic. The people with the knives, thank goodness, are not coming from Gaza. Gaza is essentially walled off to Israel. The people with the knives are coming from the West Bank. So what you do in Gaza is not going to prevent the people with the knives.

If you want to prevent the people with the knives, I would respectfully suggest the Israeli Government should complete the security fence and create borders that——

Mr. PERRY. That is what they can do. But what we can do is stop funding the training camps that would be described as our elementary schools, our daycares, our middle schools, right?

Mr. WEXLER. Yes.

Mr. PERRY. We are funding that.

Mr. WEXLER. And I am deeply troubled by it.

Mr. PERRY. Troubled?

Mr. WEXLER. Yeah.

Mr. PERRY. You got to be more than—with all due respect, sir——

Mr. WEXLER. Yes.

Mr. PERRY [continuing]. We are all troubled, right? We are talking about action here. This hearing is about the funding of terrorism——

Mr. WEXLER. Yes.

Mr. PERRY [continuing]. Taxpayer funding, and that is why I asked the question.

Mr. WEXLER. That is right. Yes.

Mr. PERRY. So while we talk about platitudes here and we are all troubled—and we all are, rightfully so, yourself included—we have an opportunity here to do something.

Mr. WEXLER. And all I would suggest is, if you are going to do that—which, obviously, your bill stands for that—then at least have round two figured out on how you are going to achieve your purpose, which is minimize terrorism, not enhance it.

So, yes, if you are taking that first step, which may be very legitimate, figure out step two, which is, as the followup, how are you actually reducing terrorism as opposed to creating an even greater incentive.

Mr. PERRY. With all due respect, sir, I hear what you are saying, but the policy that comes to—and I thank your indulgence, Mr.

Chairman—what I see as appeasement at some point, that it is my duty, that it is my duty to figure out how to solve that problem or I must pay some blood money, extortion, seems counterintuitive to every moral code that I have ever followed in my life.

Mr. WEXLER. And, if I may, I couldn't agree with you more. And I would just respectfully suggest that, before you reach your ultimate conclusion, you sit down with our Egyptian allies and our Israeli allies and our Jordanian allies and ask them what their suggestions would be for round two to make sure you don't make the——

Mr. PERRY. Maybe round one can be a forcing function.

Thank you, Mr. Chairman. I yield back.

Chairman ROYCE. Okay.

Mark Meadows from North Carolina.

Mr. MEADOWS. Thank you, Mr. Chairman. And thank you for holding this hearing. As you know, this is a passionate area for me, having cosponsored legislation that suggests that we should close the PLO office here in Washington, DC, as long as they continue to fund terrorists who commit these kinds of acts.

So, Mr. Wexler, you know, you have come up with a lot of suggestions on what the Israelis should do. Do you not think it would be a prudent call to close the PLO office here in Washington, DC, as long as we are paying terrorists to commit terrorist acts?

Mr. WEXLER. Principally——

Mr. MEADOWS. Just yes or no.

Mr. WEXLER. No, it is not that simple.

Mr. MEADOWS. It is that simple. Let me tell you——

Mr. WEXLER. No, it isn't.

Mr. MEADOWS. Let me tell you why the problem is.

Mr. WEXLER. Yeah.

Mr. MEADOWS. I have five Jewish young girls over here who don't understand. I don't understand why we can't close a PLO office when I was told by the Ambassador that they were not going to fund terrorist activities anymore. And all they did was moved it from the PLA to the PLO.

And so what we are doing is we are continuing to do it. We need to close that office. We need to make sure that what happens is at least we send a message. If we can't close an office, then we certainly cannot be serious about addressing this issue.

Mr. WEXLER. Then close it. And——

Mr. MEADOWS. Why would you not support that?

Mr. WEXLER. Because my fear—my fear is that when we take actions like the one you are describing, which are totally justifiable based on the facts of what is occurring, that, in effect, we are rewarding the terrorist inclinations amongst their society as opposed to the more pragmatic ones.

Mr. MEADOWS. But based on——

Mr. WEXLER. Remember—hold on.

Mr. MEADOWS. But based on that, based on that, your whole philosophy is a philosophy of appeasement.

Mr. WEXLER. No.

Mr. MEADOWS. Historically, that has never worked.

Mr. WEXLER. Not fair, sir. My philosophy——

Mr. MEADOWS. Well, it is fair, because what you are saying is we can't even close an office.

Mr. WEXLER. My philosophy is the philosophy of the Mossad. My philosophy is the philosophy of the Shin Bet——

Mr. MEADOWS. All right. But——

Mr. WEXLER [continuing]. The roughest Israeli fighters.

Mr. MEADOWS. Mr. Wexler, let me come back.

Mr. WEXLER. Who is——

Mr. MEADOWS. Hold on. It is my time.

Mr. WEXLER. You are correct.

Mr. MEADOWS. So let me come back. Because I was on the ground in Israel when the latest round of stabbings occurred. And for you to sit here and suggest that somehow this is a goodwill tour, that the Israelis are going to be viewed in a positive light if they just give a little bit more—I was there when Western papers were talking about how it was the Jewish boy's fault that he was stabbed and not the Palestinian. I was there when he was doing the ISIS sign from his hospital bed, when they said that the Israelis had killed him, which was not the fact. I was there on the ground.

And so to suggest that somehow building a wall will fix this problem? I can tell you, if the Israeli Government felt like building a wall will bring peace, it would be built quicker than any wall you could ever see. But that will not do it because you and I both know that the Palestinians go back and forth between those walls.

I was in a courtroom——

Mr. WEXLER. Sir——

Mr. MEADOWS. I was in a courtroom where I had a Hamas attorney with Palestinian youth that were prideful of the fact that they had committed these atrocities, as if they had won a spelling bee. How do we change that?

Mr. WEXLER. With all due respect, Israel was suffering from suicide bombs every week, blowing themselves up left and right, under Prime Minister Sharon. What was his primary response? He built the wall that was highly controversial internationally—the Palestinians opposed to it, most of the international operators opposed to it. But Sharon went and built the wall. And guess what? Israel, to the degree—again, it is relative—defeated the intifada, in great part because of that wall.

So, with all due respect——

Mr. MEADOWS. Well, with all due respect——

Mr. WEXLER [continuing]. You can't say a wall won't help. It does help——

Mr. MEADOWS. No, no.

Mr. WEXLER [continuing]. Greatly. In fact——

Mr. MEADOWS. I didn't say it wouldn't help. What I said, it would not solve the problem.

Mr. WEXLER. You are correct. It won't.

Mr. MEADOWS. Those were my exact words.

Mr. WEXLER. It won't solve the problem.

Mr. MEADOWS. And what I am here today to say is, if we can't take minor steps like closing a PLO office, then what are we supposed to tell the generations to come? That we would not even take small, diplomatic—I mean, we are not talking about cutting off their funds. All we are saying is they can't have an office here in Washington, DC. Does that not seem like a reasonable compromise?

Mr. WEXLER. It is. It is reasonable.

Mr. MEADOWS. Then why don't you support it?

Mr. WEXLER. Because I would just simply ask the question, the day after you close it, have you benefited Hamas and the more extreme elements, or have you changed the behavior and sent a message?

Mr. MEADOWS. Well, we know that what we have been doing didn't work. We know that they continue to pay terrorists. At what point do we change our philosophy to figure out if some new strategy would work?

I will yield back.

Chairman ROYCE. Okay. We go to Mr. Brad Sherman of California.

Mr. SHERMAN. Thank you.

Rob, welcome back. You may be having more fun in that seat than you had in the seats on this side.

It has been suggested that maybe we should have a change in American policy and we should have an American President who declares that we are neutral between Israel and its enemies and that the upside of that would be that somehow that neutral President would be able to create peace just by convening a meeting.

What are the dangers of the United States declaring that we are neutral but available to have discussions between Israel and its enemies?

And if the United States was not a stalwart friend of Israel, would Panama be the most powerful nation that Israel could count on as a stalwart friend, or would there be some other nation that would rise to the top as being on Israel's side?

Mr. WEXLER. I think you raise a very valid point. Neutrality by the United States with respect to Israel and its neighbors would be catastrophic. It would be catastrophic for Israel, it would be catastrophic for America.

Quite frankly, I have never understood the term ''honest broker.'' I don't understand why we Americans would ever even suggest that Americais an honest broker. We are a strong ally of Israel because of shared values, because of democratic values, because of a whole host of moral, ethical, common ties. And the fact that Israel is our closest ally in the Middle East, it would be catastrophic if the world perceived that we moved even slightly away from that very strong position.

And what is even stronger is events like what occurred 2 weeks ago, where the Israeli military establishment—I think they were in Texas, or I forget where—where the F-35 Strike Fighter plane was delivered effectively to Israel, rightfully so. And they are the only country in the region that has that next-generation American technology.

That sends the right message both to Israel's opponents and also to our other allies in the region, our Arab allies and elsewise, to encourage them to engage more substantially with Israel.

Mr. SHERMAN. I would point out that Israel does not lack for honest brokers. Every former Prime Minister of Britain has offered himself as an honest broker, not to mention everyone who imagines themselves winning an Nobel Peace Prize. There is no shortage of honest brokers. Israel does have a shortage of stalwart friends, which is why if we were not among them I hesitate to think who would be at the top of the list.

The Israeli Ministry of Education and the municipality of Jerusalem now allow new versions of the Palestinian textbooks to be used in East Jerusalem. The Palestinian Authority has claimed that they are taking out of those textbooks incitements to violence.

Have they achieved this with regard to these new textbooks, both for those being used in Jerusalem and those being used in the West Bank and Gaza?

Mr. Wexler?

Mr. WEXLER. My understanding is that, unfortunately, they have not achieved any dramatic reduction in the incitement contained in the textbooks. My understanding is there have been certain changes made that are moving in the right direction, but I don't think anyone here would categorize those as even nearly sufficient enough.

Mr. SHERMAN. And I would point out that we could reduce the amount of money we give the Palestinian Authority and give them textbooks, in which case we would make sure that there would be no incitement in those textbooks.

I will ask the other two witnesses, are you familiar with these textbooks, the new version, and how would you apprise them?

Mr. Carmon?

Mr. CARMON. We are working on this, and we will publish a report about the new textbook.

Mr. SHERMAN. Can you give us a preview? It will help sales. Go on.

Mr. CARMON. The previous one was simply the textbooks of the Palestinian Authority and Jordan, a mixture of both. Unfortunately, the Israeli Government turned a blind eye to all that, and now it is changing its position.

But, you know, when Abbas declares the prisoners are our top priority, this is a message. The money is not coming as some social welfare. It is ideological money. It conveys a message that the fight is the top priority, even though we are not doing it for now. But it is in violation of Oslo, and from Oslo they got the recognition from all the other nations. So I don't expect——

Mr. SHERMAN. I will just point out, if you give the PA cash, you don't know how they will spend it. If you give them textbooks, we at least know that they can't be misused. Whether they will be actually used, I don't know.

And, Mr. Chairman, I believe my time has expired.

Chairman ROYCE. Your time has expired, but I must confess that is a good idea, to supplant the textbooks with the funding and other forms of education.

Let me go then to Mr. Ted Yoho of Florida. Thank you.

Mr. YOHO. Thank you, Mr. Chairman.

And I appreciate the panel being here.

And I think that is good idea, to follow up on textbooks.

Let's see. The meeting today was ''Financially Rewarding Terrorism in the West Bank.'' And that is exactly what we see with the Palestinian Authority. I have been here for 3½ years, and it amazes me—because we talk about this—that we are rewarding terrorist activities.

We put in a resolution a year and a half ago, Resolution 542, that would cease and stop all payments to the Palestinian Authority until they stopped doing what they are doing.

And, you know, I have heard the arguments on both sides of this. "If we stop this, it will open up a vacuum; that vacuum will get filled by worse players." For 3½ years, I have sat here and watched this discussion, and since 2008 we have given approximately $500 million a year to the Palestinian Authority in the name of peace. The American people are being sold that we are giving this foreign aid to the Palestinian Authority in the name of peace—$4 billion, $4 billion of my money, of everybody sitting here's money.

Every person in America has paid $4 billion in the name of peace, yet the Palestinian Authority, through their own laws, which I find—they have a National Palestinian Fund. And it goes on to say, "Financial support for prisoners is anchored in a series of laws and government decrees. The prisoners are described as a fighting sector. The financial rights"—the financial rights—"of the prisoner and his family must be assured." "The financial rights of the prisoner and his family must be assured."

It also stated that the PA will provide allowance to every prisoner without discrimination. Well, I am glad to see they don't discriminate. According to the law, the PA must—must—provide prisoners with a monthly allowance during their incarceration and salaries or jobs upon release. They are also entitled to exemptions from payments for education, health care, and professional training.

Years of imprisonment are calculated as years of seniority of service in PA institutions. Whoever is in prison for 5 years or more is entitled to a job in the PA institution. The PA gives priority in job placement to people who were involved in terrorist activities.

Does this sound like a policy to bring peace? Does anybody want to just make a quick comment? Because I want to go on.

Mr. Wexler.

Mr. WEXLER. The payments to the terrorists and their families are indefensible. A policy for peace, though, is also what we have done relatively successfully in terms of training Palestinian security forces, which today are the forces that work with the Israeli Government to maintain a greater degree of security in the West Bank.

Mr. YOHO. Okay. I hear that. And when we put in this resolution, we got some blow-back from the Jewish community saying this would be terrible, it would increase more violence.

And it reminds me of that essay that was written—I am sure you guys have heard of it—"The Sheep, the Wolves, and the Sheepdogs." It was written by a retired Army lieutenant colonel, David Grossman. And they said there is a certain amount of risk that people are willing to live with. And when the sheep knows his enemy is the wolf, they will huddle to one side of the pasture because they understand there is a certain amount of risk. They are not going to get everybody. But they will live with that. But when you introduce an unknown, the sheepdog, the sheep don't understand that it is there to protect them, so they run over to the wolf, their known enemy.

And I think that we have a situation here that we know that we are giving money in the name of peace. We have a history of doing that. And it is not working. And the unknown is what happens if we remove that.

And I want to build on what my colleague Mr. Perry said, that I think it would change people's focus and they would have to pivot and say, you know what, the Americans are playing hardball—I don't want to say "hardball," but very discrete, or very direct, and say, if these policies continue, we are done.

You know, the textbooks, as Mr. Sherman brought up, I have heard that for 3 years. We are funding hatred. We are funding terrorism. And I think if we, as Americans, as the government, come out strongly and say our new policy is this, you need to make adjustments in the Palestinian Authority and in Israel, because we are not going to tolerate this anymore.

You know, I don't need to remind anybody in here, our Government is struggling financially. To spend $6 billion in the name of peace, when we can't pay our own veterans and we can't do things here, I think is unconscionable. And I will not support any money going to the Palestinian Authority.

Thank you.

Chairman ROYCE. Thank you.

We go now to Brendan Boyle of Pennsylvania.

Mr. BOYLE. Thank you, Mr. Chairman. And as I have said previously, the way that you and Mr. Engel lead this committee on issues as they relate to Israel's security is admirable and reflects the best spirit of bipartisanship when it comes to foreign affairs for the United States.

Just in reflecting on what has been going on recently, the 300 or so wounded, the 30 Israelis that have been killed in these knifing attacks, what has been going on now is essentially the slow-motion intifada that, unfortunately, has not gotten as much attention around the world as it should.

And I think that a real turning point was clearly the—everyone talks about Camp David that succeeded in the late seventies. But, really, you could say the one that had the more effect was the failed Camp David attempt in 2000, which was building up to be the culmination of the Oslo process and a two-state solution, recognition on both sides, and resolving most of the outstanding issues.

And when Yasser Arafat walked away from that and went back to Ramallah and launched the intifada, it has led exactly to where we are today in 2016, 16 years later. And so many people have lost their lives and been wounded.

And so now here we are, in the West and especially the United States, trying to get the parties back to an agreement that, if you read, say, Dennis Ross' account of it or even Bill Clinton's autobiography, it is pretty clear that, whether it be next year or 20 years from now, we are probably going to get a final resolution that looks a lot more like the 2000 Camp David attempt than not.

So, in terms of getting back to that and how we get back on track and recognizing the current configuration of the Israeli Government and an 85-year-old Mahmoud Abbas who is seemingly not interested in peace at all, I want to return to something that was discussed earlier, and that is the Arab Peace Initiative. Because one advantage of the whole—wherever anyone stood on the Iranian deal, one unexpected, positive, unintended consequence was greater cooperation between Israel and its Arab neighbors.

Could that be the genesis of a renewed Arab-led peace initiative that would put pressure on the Palestinian leadership to finally come to the table? For any of you.

Dr. Pollock? And then we can go down the table.

Mr. POLLOCK. All right, thank you. Thank you for the question. I would start by saying I hope so but I am skeptical. I think it would be in the interest of Arab governments to do exactly what you suggest, but I think that they don't see it that way. They see it, unfortunately, as risky, at least in the short term, and——

Mr. BOYLE. Internally risky——

Mr. POLLOCK. Yes.

Mr. BOYLE [continuing]. With their own domestic political situation?

Mr. POLLOCK. Yes, internally risky. And probably they also see it as risky internationally, in the sense of they are not sure what they would get for pushing the Palestinians back to the table, either from Israel, from the United States, from the international community, and so on.

And so I think that, without getting our hopes up too high, it would be worth trying—as I suggested in my written statement and briefly in my testimony today, it would be worth it for the United States to try to explore with some of our Arab allies under what conditions and with what expectations and for what returns they would be willing to do exactly what you suggested, put pressure on the Palestinians to go back to the table.

There was some sense that I had that President Sisi of Egypt, for example, about a month or so ago was preparing to do that, and then he seemed to stop because his sense of possible changes in the Israeli Government did not materialize.

Today, as I said in my comments earlier, unfortunately, some Arab governments that were more flexible about this 2 or 3 years ago have walked that back. And you now have, for example, the Saudi Foreign Minister, Adel al-Jubeir, stating in Paris, where he shouldn't have been in the first place, for that ill-advised so-called peace conference, stating that the Arab Peace Initiative was unchangeable, that they would not negotiate any amendments to it or show any flexibility about it.

That, as I said, is walking back a previous position. But if you walk it back in the wrong direction, maybe, just maybe, the United States can encourage the Saudis or other Arab governments to walk back the walk-back in the right direction, which would mean offering Israel a peace initiative to negotiate, not to impose.

Mr. BOYLE. Mr. Carmon?

Mr. CARMON. So thank you for this question because it is a crucial one. What holds back the peace process or the chances to move ahead? The Arab peace plan, in its original form when the Saudis suggested it, did not include the right of return, which is a nonstarter. Later, in a meeting of the Arab League, it was included and, thus, became the Arab peace plan.

With the right of return, of course, nothing can happen. And if it is unchangeable, then there is no change in the Arab position. Only with a change on this point can there be anything moving ahead.

And this is also the position of Abbas. Why everything stopped? Because he insists on the right of return. When Prime Minister Olmert suggested 100 percent of the territory through swap of land, what remained there to be holding it back? Only the demand for the right of return.

So, unfortunately, the Arab peace plan is a non-starter as long as it is unchangeable. And the tragedy of it is that the Saudi Foreign Minister said it, while the Saudis, who initiated it—and, in their initial suggestion, it did not include the right of return.

Mr. WEXLER. If I may, Mr. Chairman?

Chairman ROYCE. Mr. Wexler.

Mr. WEXLER. I think the proper construct is this. And your point is excellent. From 1948 until the Israeli-Egyptian Peace Treaty, the entire focus of the region was regional war against Israel. When Israel made peace with Egypt, the prospect of regional war diminished substantially. When Jordan and Israel made peace in 1993-1994, the likelihood of regional war essentially was extinguished.

With the Arab Peace Initiative, I think both Dr. Pollock and Mr. Carmon are correct, but I don't think that should be the ultimate message. Yes, skepticism; yes, look at the fine print, and it is not where it needs to be. But with the advent of the Arab Peace Initiative, we went from the reality of regional war against Israel to the prospect—in its infancy, admittedly—the prospect of regional peace.

Now, where I would beg to differ with Mr. Carmon is, in looking at the language of the right of return in the Arab Peace Initiative, is it where Israel would need it to be to ultimately agree? Of course not. But the actual language is ''just and agreed.'' And the Arab position—and I am not suggesting we accept it, but the Arab position is that, by adding the word ''agreed,'' they were recognizing that there would be no right of return unless Israel agreed. And, of course, Israel would never agree to hundreds of thousands of Palestinians coming into Israel, so, therefore, they were making a concession.

Whether it is true or not is not the point. The point is it is an opening. It is an opening that should be explored.

And, with all due respect, saying that we know that the Arab Peace Initiative is not amendable or not changeable—well, we know it is, because they came a year and a half ago or 2 years ago and made a change, in terms of they went from ''1967 lines'' to ''1967 lines with limited territorial swaps.'' Again, not where the Israelis need to be, but movement in the correct direction.

Chairman ROYCE. Okay. Mr. Ron DeSantis of Florida is next.

Mr. DESANTIS. Thank you, Mr. Chairman.

I thank the witnesses.

This is really a frustrating issue because we have been raising it time and time again, and I really appreciate, Mr. Carmon, your testimony laying it out. These are huge payments that are going to Palestinian terrorists. When you start talking about people who have committed really heinous acts and they are raking in $3,100 a month, for a Palestinian Arab, that has to be better than 99 percent of the people who don't have access, who don't own an oil field in the whole Middle East. So that is major, major money.

And what that evidences is an unambiguous policy to promote terrorism. It is really no different than what this committee rightfully will criticize the Government of Iran for doing, sponsoring terrorism. And this Congress has responded to that with sanctions in a variety of contexts to counteract Iran's policy of support for terrorism. And we really have something similar here, and I think we need to act to try to change the policy.

Mr. Carmon, you made the point, in 2014 there was the policy change, that these payments no longer came from the Palestinian Authority and they are done from the PLO. Why did they make that change?

Mr. CARMON. It was under the pressure of donor countries.

Mr. DeSANTIS. Because the donor countries don't want to be accused of funding the payments to terrorism.

Mr. CARMON. Absolutely.

Mr. DeSANTIS. However, money is fungible. There is a certain amount of things they have to do. So if you then say the terror payments will come out of the PLO, that just means that some of the money that the PA is getting will go to other things. If that money was removed, because you are still funding terrorists and you are still paying them, then they would have to make decisions.

And so I don't think that any of these countries can have a clear conscience simply because they have kind of shuffled the deck chairs around a little bit and are saying, well, no, it is actually not from the PA. This is all being worked together.

And I think that this is one example, but correct me if I'm wrong—I think your organization has reported on this. Doesn't the Palestinian Authority lionize terrorists by doing things like naming parks and sports stadiums after them?

Mr. CARMON. Definitely. The message is respect— legitimatization, respect, and even hero-ization of those who are involved in these acts.

Mr. DeSANTIS. And I also note, I know there are varying views of Mr. Abbas on this panel for sure, on the Foreign Affairs Committee, but this is a guy whose dissertation was in Holocaust denial. And you can say that he is not as bad as some of the other guys, like Hamas or whatever, but this is not necessarily somebody who is a full-fledged supporter of a lasting peace.

And I think incitement has really become endemic to this culture. You look at not only the textbook, some of the programming, and the viciousness with which they attack Jews, particularly Israeli Jews, but people that are different from them, I think is just absolutely horrifying.

And I was very, very disgusted to see, after this Tel Aviv attack in June, brutal attack at this cafe, you had people in the Gaza Strip, Palestinian Arabs, and in the West Bank, they were cheering that. Isn't that correct, Mr. Carmon? That was cause for celebration?

Mr. CARMON. There was, yes.

Mr. DeSANTIS. So I appreciate a lot of the comments that we have heard. I know there is this complicated issue, there are a lot of things. But, to me, the overriding problem is the behavior of not just the Palestinian Authority or Hamas per se, but really the majority impulse in the culture is one that simply does not recognize Israel's right to exist as a Jewish state and really doesn't seek a two-state solution, to the extent they want that as something for a lasting peace, but really as one step in the direction to ultimately seek Israel's destruction.

And until those underlying dynamics change, I don't think you are going to see a lot of possibility to—because here is the thing. There is difference of opinion in Israel, but the Israeli population has showed time and time again they are willing to make very significant concessions to achieve a lasting peace. And I have no doubt about that. And I know people can criticize this policy or that policy coming out of the government. But that is just, to me, unquestioned. It is not even close that the Palestinian Arabs have demonstrated that in any type of broad sense.

So here we are with the funding issue. I don't think we can allow tax dollars to be going to this entity knowing that they are working in cahoots with the PLO and that these payments are being made. Not only is it when you subsidize something, you are going to get more of terrorism, but it is also just the moral blot of any entity that wants to reward this type of activity, I think, is something that we absolutely cannot have anything to do with.

So I really appreciate the chairman calling the hearing. I have enjoyed listening to all the witnesses and their testimony. And I yield back.

Mr. POLLOCK. Mr. Chairman?

Chairman ROYCE. Yes, Dr. Pollock.

Mr. POLLOCK. Yes, if I may, I know that we have used up a lot of time. I want to just end with this comment on my own behalf.

I would suggest trying to be constructive. If we can perhaps reach a consensus that the money that the PA uses to fund terrorists and terrorism should be deducted from the taxpayer support that the United States provides to them, perhaps at the same time it could be transferred to the kinds of activities that I suggested that would be constructive for both Israel and the PA, for Israelis and Palestinians to support—for example, an international fund that would enable people-to-people and interfaith dialogue and cooperative activities between Israelis and Palestinians on the ground. I think that kind of approach might have the virtue of not being purely punitive but also constructive.

Thank you.

Chairman ROYCE. Mr. Carmon?

Mr. CARMON. I believe that this money is ideological money. It reflects an ideology which we see in the insistence on the right of return.

I would also like to be positive and suggest that the main focus of U.S. foreign policy would be in this respect on demanding of the PLO to stop with this nonstarter. Mr. Abbas sent his special envoy to the Herzliya conference just a few weeks ago, Mr. Ahmad Majdalani, who said there all refugees must go back to their ''homes.'' So this is the position, and the money is just a reflection of it. This is what has to be changed, and of course the money too.

Chairman ROYCE. And Mr. Wexler.

Mr. WEXLER. Well, first, Mr. Chairman, I want to thank you for what I think has been a terrific discussion, and thank you for doing it.

On the funding question itself, I think we must reiterate, though, that the State Department did, if I understand it correctly, cut $80 million in Fiscal Year 2015 to the Palestinian Authority. So maybe—not ''maybe''—if this committee wants to achieve its purpose, then it needs to broaden the universe in which our funding is not allowed to go ultimately, one way or another, and maybe there is language that can accomplish that purpose.

There is no representative of the Palestinian Government here, and I am surely the furthest thing from it. However—and we rightfully condemn their heinous actions. This is a good example, in terms of the funding.

But on the right of return, this record would be incomplete if it did not include the fact that Mr. Abbas, President Abbas, when asked—his hometown is Safed, if I understand it correctly. And when he was asked on a public show whether his intention was to return to his hometown, he said, ''Yes, as a visitor. And I understand I won't live there forever.'' And then I understand, afterward, he dialed it back and made it in language that might be more agreeable to many in his own population.

I am not trying to color it one way or the other. The point I am only trying to make is these are questions of degree. As unsatisfactory as they are, they need to be negotiated at the negotiation table.

And I would close with this. Our ultimate goal should be to create a dynamic in which the Israelis and the Palestinians can agree to a two-state outcome. In the interim, we should encourage those independent steps that preserve the likelihood or the ability to achieve a two-state outcome when the politics of the region allow those two groups to get there.

Chairman ROYCE. Well, we appreciate the time of our witnesses today.

As we have heard, if we are to have a real chance at peace, the practice—and this is my focus—this practice of financially rewarding terror in the West Bank must stop. And that includes conversations with Europeans and others. But, internationally, it is a nonstarter to have a circumstance in which this slaughter continues and it is aided and abetted by a system that is paying people and teaching people how to carry out murder, how to slay others.

And I again thank our witnesses.

And, at this point, we stand adjourned.

[Whereupon, at 12:37 p.m., the committee was adjourned.]

APPENDIX

MATERIAL SUBMITTED FOR THE RECORD

FULL COMMITTEE HEARING NOTICE
COMMITTEE ON FOREIGN AFFAIRS
U.S. HOUSE OF REPRESENTATIVES
WASHINGTON, DC 20515-6128

Edward R. Royce (R-CA), Chairman

July 6, 2016

TO: MEMBERS OF THE COMMITTEE ON FOREIGN AFFAIRS

You are respectfully requested to attend an OPEN hearing of the Committee on Foreign Affairs, to be held in Room 2172 of the Rayburn House Office Building (and available live on the Committee website at http://www.ForeignAffairs.house.gov):

DATE: Wednesday, July 6, 2016

TIME: 10:00 a.m.

SUBJECT: Financially Rewarding Terrorism in the West Bank

WITNESSES: David Pollock, Ph.D.
                   Kaufman Fellow
                   Washington Institute for Near East Policy

                   Mr. Yigal Carmon
                   President and Founder
                   Middle East Media Research Institute

                   The Honorable Robert Wexler
                   President
                   S. Daniel Abraham Center for Middle East Peace

By Direction of the Chairman

The Committee on Foreign Affairs seeks to make its facilities accessible to persons with disabilities. If you are in need of special accommodations, please call 202/225-5021 at least four business days in advance of the event, whenever practicable. Questions with regard to special accommodations in general (including availability of Committee materials in alternative formats and assistive listening devices) may be directed to the Committee.

COMMITTEE ON FOREIGN AFFAIRS
MINUTES OF FULL COMMITTEE HEARING

Day _Wednesday_ Date _7/6/2016_ Room _2172_

Starting Time _10:13_ Ending Time _12:37_

Recesses | _0_ | (___to___) (___to___) (___to___) (___to___) (___to___) (___to___)

Presiding Member(s)

Chairman Edward R. Royce

Check all of the following that apply:

Open Session ☑
Executive (closed) Session ☐
Televised ☑

Electronically Recorded (taped) ☑
Stenographic Record ☑

TITLE OF HEARING:

Financially Rewarding Terrorism in the West Bank

COMMITTEE MEMBERS PRESENT:

See attached.

NON-COMMITTEE MEMBERS PRESENT:

none

HEARING WITNESSES: Same as meeting notice attached? Yes ☑ No ☐
(If "no", please list below and include title, agency, department, or organization.)

STATEMENTS FOR THE RECORD: _(List any statements submitted for the record.)_

IFR - Rep. Dan Donovan
IFR - Rep. Eliot Engel
IFR - Rep. Lois Frankel
SFR - Rep. Ileana Ros-Lehtinen
SFR - Rep. Gerald Connolly

TIME SCHEDULED TO RECONVENE _____
or
TIME ADJOURNED _12:37_

Jean Marter, Director of Committee Operations

HOUSE COMMITTEE ON FOREIGN AFFAIRS
FULL COMMITTEE HEARING

PRESENT	MEMBER
X	Edward R. Royce, CA
	Christopher H. Smith, NJ
	Ileana Ros-Lehtinen, FL
X	Dana Rohrabacher, CA
X	Steve Chabot, OH
X	Joe Wilson, SC
	Michael T. McCaul, TX
	Ted Poe, TX
X	Matt Salmon, AZ
	Darrell Issa, CA
	Tom Marino, PA
X	Jeff Duncan, SC
X	Mo Brooks, AL
	Paul Cook, CA
X	Randy Weber, TX
X	Scott Perry, PA
X	Ron DeSantis, FL
X	Mark Meadows, NC
X	Ted Yoho, FL
	Curt Clawson, FL
	Scott DesJarlais, TN
	Reid Ribble, WI
	Dave Trott, MI
X	Lee Zeldin, NY
X	Dan Donovan, NY

PRESENT	MEMBER
X	Eliot L. Engel, NY
X	Brad Sherman, CA
	Gregory W. Meeks, NY
X	Albio Sires, NJ
X	Gerald E. Connolly, VA
	Theodore E. Deutch, FL
	Brian Higgins, NY
X	Karen Bass, CA
X	William Keating, MA
	David Cicilline, RI
	Alan Grayson, FL
X	Ami Bera, CA
	Alan S. Lowenthal, CA
X	Grace Meng, NY
X	Lois Frankel, FL
	Tulsi Gabbard, HI
X	Joaquin Castro, TX
X	Robin Kelly, IL
X	Brendan Boyle, PA

Material submitted for the record by the Honorable Daniel Donovan, a Representative in Congress from the State of New York

The Union of Orthodox Jewish Congregations of America
820 First Street, NE, Suite 730 • Washington, D.C. 20002
Tel: 202-513-6484 • Fax: 202-513-6497 • E-mail: info@ouadvocacy.org

---

House Foreign Affairs Committee
Hearing: Financially Rewarding Terrorism in the West Bank
Wednesday, July 6, 2016

Statement for the Record
Nathan Diament, Executive Director for Public Policy, Union of Orthodox Jewish Congregations of America

Chairman Royce, Ranking Member Engel, and Members of the House Foreign Affairs Committee, thank you for holding today's hearing on *Israel, the Palestinian Authority, and Barriers to Peace.* On behalf of the Union of Orthodox Jewish Congregations of America (Orthodox Union)—the nation's largest Orthodox Jewish umbrella organization—I am pleased to submit this statement for the record.

Unfortunately, the timing of this hearing is searing and salient as we mourn the loss last week of 13-year-old Hallel Ariel, an Israeli girl stabbed to death by a teenaged Palestinian terrorist as she slept in her home, and of Rabbi Miki Mark, who on July 1 was shot to death as he drove with his family. Since September of last year, Palestinian terrorists perpetuated nearly 300 other stabbings, shootings, and vehicular assaults against Israelis. It is time for the United States Congress to take concrete action to impose consequences upon a Palestinian leadership that enables the murder of innocent people.

Last week, even before the tragic murder of young Hallel, the Senate Appropriations Committee included in the State and Foreign Operations Appropriations Act--on a bipartisan vote--a provision to restrict U.S. taxpayer dollars to funds that support payments to Palestinians and their families who commit terrorist attacks. I urge the House of Representatives to join their colleagues in the Senate to ensure that U.S. financial aid does not go toward funding terrorists or their families.

According to a 2015 Congressional Research Service report, the Palestinians are among the largest recipients of international aid, with the U.S. contributing more than $5 billion in security assistance and bilateral economic aid since the mid-1990s. In addition, the U.S. Agency for International Development and the U.S. supported United Nations Relief and Works Agency for Palestinian Refugees in the Near East provide hundreds of millions of indirect economic assistance for humanitarian programs, education, medical care, vocational training, and other initiatives.

A key purpose of this aid, which is traditionally supported by the Government of Israel, is to enable Palestinian Authority (PA) forces to stop Palestinian terrorist attacks against Israelis. However, since September 2015, over 300 Palestinian terrorist attacks against Israelis have occurred, resulting in 40 deaths and more than 500 wounded. Given these statistics, it is time to reexamine U.S. financial aid to the PA.

The Union of Orthodox Jewish Congregations of America
820 First Street, NE, Suite 730 • Washington, D.C. 20002
Tel: 202-513-6484 Fax: 202-513-6497 E-mail: info@ouadvocacy.org

Exacerbating these matters is the evidence that the PA has been using U.S. funds to pay stipends to the families of thousands of Palestinians who are committing the terror attacks. Palestinian terrorist prisoners are regarded by the PA as patriotic "fighters" and as employees of the government of the PA. While in prison, these terrorists and their families are paid premium salaries and given extra benefits as rewards for their service. According to a recent report from the Gatestone Institute, "terrorists in prison receive higher average salary than PA civil servants and military personnel." And a 2014 study by the Israeli government, based on internal PA documents, showed that these "prisoners" and their families had received more than $75 million in stipends in just one year.

Upon release from custody, the terrorists become civil service employees. Shockingly, monthly salaries for both incarcerated and released prisoners are on a sliding scale, depending on the severity of the crime and length of prison sentence.

The United States Department of State, in its 2015 Terrorism Report, confirmed the payments to terrorists, stating, "As part of a policy codified in 2003, the PA provided significant financial packages to Palestinian security prisoners released from Israeli prisons in 2014 in an effort to reintegrate them into society…" The Terrorism Report further found that PA social media websites have posted pro-terrorism messages, including the posting of political cartoons glorifying stabbing attacks.

When violent attacks occur in Israel, like the one against 13-year-old Hallel, there is no doubt that such violence is the result of the incessant incitement against Israelis that is spread by Palestinian leadership. It is time for U.S. leaders to not only clearly condemn such attacks, as the State Department did last week, but to also assign responsibility properly and take the necessary steps against a Palestinian leadership that supports such atrocities.

I urge members of the Foreign Affairs Committee and the United States Congress as a whole to take immediate action. It is time to end American support—financial or otherwise—of any organization, including the PA, that supports and promotes terrorism.

The Union of Orthodox Jewish Congregations of America
820 First Street, NE, Suite 730 • Washington, D.C. 20002
Tel: 202-513-6484 Fax: 202-513-6497 E-mail: info@ouadvocacy.org

Alliance for Middle East Peace

1725 I Street, NW, Suite 300
Washington, DC 20006

(202) 618-4600 (phone)
(888) 784-4540 (fax)
info@alimep.org

Statement for the Record
House Foreign Affairs Committee

Financially Rewarding Terrorism in the West Bank
July 6, 2016

Chairman Royce and Ranking Member Engel,

The Alliance for Middle East Peace (ALLMEP) thanks you for holding this important hearing. ALLMEP is a network of ninety-three peace and reconciliation groups working on coexistence and cooperative activities between Jews and Arabs, Israelis and Palestinians.

Just last week, the Middle East Quartet issued a report on the Palestinian-Israeli conflict. The report recommends, among other things, that both sides foster a climate of tolerance, including through increasing interaction and cooperation in a variety of fields – economic, professional, educational, cultural – that strengthen the foundations for peace and countering extremism. We welcome the Quartet report and are thankful to Quartet principles for recognizing the critical work of civil society.

The work of the United States in the region is essential to our collective wish for peace in the Middle East and our entire community is deeply thankful for the commitment of the United States to its longstanding goal of finding a peaceful solution to the Israeli-Palestinian conflict.

As we look at the strategic barriers preventing the advancement of peace between Israelis and Palestinians, sadly, we see a new generation growing up who are more skeptical and less hopeful then the generation who came before them.

As we look at the most recent joint polling of Israelis and Palestinians, 56 percent of Israelis are worried or very worried on a daily basis that they will be murdered by Arabs. 79 percent of Palestinians are worried or very worried on a daily basis that they will be murdered or have their land confiscated by Jews.

It gets worse.

56 percent of Palestinians believe that the Israeli objective is to expel them from the land, 25 percent that the objective is annexation, while 43 percent of Israelis believe that all Arabs are out to kill them, and 18 percent believe their aim is the conquest of Israel and the removal of their citizenship.

Together, 60-80 percent of the two populations believe that the intent of the other is the removal of their rights or their actual destruction.

Standing against this fear and distrust is the people-to-people movement, those within society who strive to humanize Jews and Arabs, Israelis and Palestinians by building the necessary trust between the two populations.

80 ORGANIZATIONS. THOUSANDS OF ISRAELIS AND PALESTINIANS. ONE GROWING MOVEMENT FOR PEACE

We are thankful to the tremendous work of the United States Agency for International Development through its Conflict Management and Mitigation (CMM) Program. For the past eight years, the CMM Program has worked on fostering organizations that support people-to-people interactions in every societal sphere.

One program that touches both the civic and economic sphere is the Olive Oil Without Borders project run by our member, the Near East Foundation, which celebrates its centennial this year. With a CMM Program grant, Olive Oil Without Borders created relationships between Israeli and Palestinian olive oil farmers to increase income, profitability, cross-border trade, and trust among Palestinian and Israeli olive oil producers. Seeing an overcapacity of production in the Palestinian territories, the program helped facilitate a cross-border trade agreement resulting in the sale of 3,600 metric tons of olive oil and leading to increased economic collaboration between Israelis and Palestinians.

The success of Olive Oil Without Borders demonstrates just one of the positive impacts of these programs.

Kids4Peace is another example of a grantee, working to bring together the youth of East and West Jerusalem in after school activities. Over 350 families currently take part and for each place, five more families want to participate within the program. As one of the only programs linking the East and West side of Jerusalem today, it targets the very youth who are being radicalized and turning to acts of violence. Kids4Peace has a 90% retention rate as the families who the program reaches in the 6th grade stay in the program as they grow up.

CMM Program grant recipients are required to demonstrate quantitative, empirical results, with monitoring and evaluation at the heart of the CMM Program. The Near East Foundation, Kids4peace and the other CMM Program grant recipients, each perform work that is essential to a sustained peaceful solution to the Israeli-Palestinian conflict.

As we look to overcome the barriers of hate and mistrust that underpin so much of the incitement, there is an option to leverage, coordinate and scale successful people-to-people programs as a way of breaking down incitement and hate. HR 1489, a bi-partisan effort by Rep. Crowley and Rep. Fortenberry offers an International Fund to ensure long term, strategic and leveraged funding to initiatives that can combat incitement and build bridges between communities based on shared interests and mutual understanding.

ALLMEP appreciates the ongoing evaluation of Congressional budgetary priorities in the face of challenging global circumstances and believes that greater investments civil society that promotes altitudinal shifts and combats hate is a strategic investment in overcoming the barriers to peace.

We look forward to continued engagement with Congress and the Administration on the vital work of the people-to-people programs in the region that are so necessary to a longstanding peace in the Middle East.

MATERIAL SUBMITTED FOR THE RECORD BY THE HONORABLE LOIS FRANKEL, A
REPRESENTATIVE IN CONGRESS FROM THE STATE OF FLORIDA

Salaries for Suicide Bombers

by **JOHN ESTERBROOK** CBS *April 3, 2002, 4:38 PM*

Iraqi President Saddam Hussein has raised the amount offered to relatives of suicide bombers from
$10,000 per family to $25,000, U.S. Defense Secretary Donald Rumsfeld said Wednesday.

Since Iraq upped its payments last month, 12 suicide bombers have successfully struck inside Israel,
including one man who killed 25 Israelis, many of them elderly, as they sat down to a meal at a hotel to
celebrate the Jewish holiday of Passover. The families of three suicide bombers said they have recently
received payments of $25,000.

Palestinians say the bombers are driven by a priceless thirst for revenge, religious zeal and dreams of
glory — not greed.

Mahmoud Safi, leader of a pro-Iraqi Palestinian group, the Arab Liberation Front, acknowledged that
the support payments for relatives make it easier for some potential bombers to make up their minds.
"Some people stop me on the street, saying if you increase the payment to $50,000 I'll do it
immediately," Safi said. He also suggested such remarks were made mostly in jest.

Saddam has said the Palestinians need weapons and money instead of peace proposals and has provided
payments throughout a year and a half of Israeli-Palestinian battles. "I saw on Iraqi TV President
Saddam saying he will continue supporting the (uprising) even if it means selling his own clothes," said
Safi.

Rumsfeld, who said earlier this week that Saddam and the Iraqi government were offering the lower
amount, elaborated on the issue at a Pentagon briefing.

"It turns out that he has raised that amount and it's $25,000 per family, not $10,000 per family,"
Rumsfeld said.

"Here is an individual who is the head of a country, Iraq, who has proudly, publicly made a decision to
go out and actively promote and finance human sacrifice for families that will have their youngsters kill
innocent men, women and children," Rumsfeld said.

Though he did not say so, he appeared to refer to the current wave of suicide bombings on Israeli
civilian targets.

"I am simply trying to let the people of Iraq understand what their leadership is doing, to let the people
of the Middle East and the rest of the world ... know what is in fact being done to arm young people and
send them out to blow up restaurants and shopping malls and pizza parlors," he said.

Rumsfeld blasted Iraq, Iran and Syria on Monday for inflaming violence in the Middle East, and said he
raised the issue of Iraq on Wednesday to suggest it was important to "recognize that there is an
infrastructure to terrorism."

Rumsfeld said Saddam had stated publicly the payment for families "if they're able to persuade a family to have their teen-ager strap explosives on them and go out and kill themselves and kill innocent men, women and children."

"He is pleased with his idea and is promoting it in the region," Rumsfeld said of Saddam. "It is a matter of public record."

Under the new Iraqi payscale, decided on March 12 during an Arab conference in Baghdad, the families of gunmen and others who die fighting the Israelis will still receive $10,000, while the relatives of suicide bombers will get $25,000.

Safi and two others from the Arab Liberation Front visit families in the northern West Bank and make the payments. "We go to every family and give them a check," he said. "We tell them that this is a gift from President Saddam and Iraq."

But Saddam is not the only one giving money. Charities from Saudi Arabia and Qatar — both U.S. allies — pay money to families of Palestinians killed in the fighting, including suicide bombers.

Rep. Ros-Lehtinen
Statement for the Record
Full Committee Hearing on Israel/PA
Wednesday, July 6, 2016 – 10:00 a.m.; 2172 Rayburn

"For over a year now, I have been trying to get the administration to reaffirm longstanding U.S. policy to veto any resolution at the UN Security Council that would impose a resolution on Israel or place an artificial timeline on negotiations: Ambassador Patterson, Ambassador Power and Secretary Kerry – each one of them refused to simply reaffirm this policy. That is problematic and raises many red flags – especially since the administration has signaled its eagerness to make its mark on the peace process. The administration must not travel down this path – the only way to a real and lasting peace is through direct negotiations, and not through an imposed solution.

I recently led a Congressional Delegation trip to Israel – and was joined by our colleague, Randy Weber – and we spoke to Prime Minister Netanyahu. The Prime Minister once again reiterated his willingness to sit down with Abu Mazen for negotiations. He even stated that he can see some benefits to some aspects of the Arab Peace Initiative as a vehicle to move forward. But there can be no progress made when the person on the other side of the negotiations refuses to even sit down and discuss a path forward without preconditions.

Abu Mazen – who is in his 11th year of a 5 year term as President of the Palestinian Authority – is both the President of the PA and the Chairman of the PLO. He continues to support incitement and he has promised to pay the salaries of terrorists and terrorists' families rather than promise the Palestinian people peace, security and a state of their own. And we've seen how this continues to play out: just last week a 13 year old girl – a dual U.S. and Israeli citizen - was stabbed to death in her sleep by a young Palestinian terrorist.

What was Abu Mazen's response? He refused to condemn the attack. In fact, his party was among the first Palestinian factions to praise and celebrate the terrorist and this heinous act. And this is the man the administration continues to push the Israelis to negotiate with? Abu Mazen, the PA and the PLO are all in violation of multiple U.S. laws, yet time and again, the administration waives these laws to allow U.S. taxpayer dollars to continue to flow to the benefit of the Palestinian leadership. This only serves to legitimize their behavior and their support for incitement and terror.

The PLO office here in Washington, DC was allowed to open after Oslo so that it could help implement Oslo and facilitate the peace process. Yet by every measurable standard, it has abjectly failed to live up to its mandate. So why then do we allow the PLO office to remain open when it is working against what we are trying to accomplish? I have introduced a bill, H.R. 4522, the PLO Accountability Act – alongside our colleague Mark Meadows from North Carolina, who has been a leader on this issue as well – that would place commonsense restrictions on the implementation of this waiver until the PLO met certain criteria.

We cannot continue to reward Abu Mazen's intransigence, his support for terror and incitement to violence, and his damaging efforts at the UN. We must demand that the administration enforce all existing laws, otherwise we will only further embolden Abu Mazen and the Palestinian leadership."

Statement for the Record
Submitted by Mr. Connolly of Virginia

It should be noted for the record that the original title of this hearing was, "Israel, the Palestinian Authority, and Barriers to Peace," which would have scoped for the House Foreign Affairs Committee a serious and timely discussion on the array of obstacles facing one of the world's most intractable active conflicts. However, the Committee was noticed of a title change that appears to narrow the focus of the hearing and gives the appearance that the Committee might be neglecting other pressing issues facing the peace process.

This observation is not meant to diminish the importance of the topic denoted by the new title. Making payments to individuals who commit crimes against the State of Israel is a detestable practice and barrier to peace that the U.S. government is right to condemn. The U.S. also counters this practice by making offsetting deductions to the assistance provided to the Palestinian Authority (PA) and uses assistance funding to make direct payments to PA creditors.

The discussion befitting of this Committee is one that seeks to identify comprehensively the barriers to peace in the Israeli-Palestinian conflict, and hopefully be a constructive participant in helping the two sides map a path forward for the peace process.

Underlying the Israeli-Palestinian conflict is a series of agreements and protocols that have sought to subdue the perceived millennia-old enmity between the two sides. From Camp David to Oslo to Wye River, the U.S. has played an integral role in the effort to broker a lasting peace in the Israeli-Palestinian conflict. Unfortunately, commitments have gone unfulfilled, and preconditions have remained obstacles to engaging in a constructive dialogue.

However, maintenance of the status quo is one of the greatest threats facing this conflict. Besieged on all sides and locked in conflict in perpetuity is not a future we should accept for the United States' closest ally in the Middle East, and no population, Israeli or Palestinian, can envision a peaceful future for the region when Palestinian communities are crippled by widespread poverty, pervasive acts terrorism, and periodic conflict that devastates local infrastructure.

On Friday, July 1, the Quartet of peace negotiators, the U.S., United Nations, European Union, and Russia, issued a report that criticized Palestinian incitement to violence and an arms build-up in Gaza as well as Israeli settlement building. Addressing these barriers to peace should be the focus of our work with the two sides. The recent rapprochement agreement between Turkey and Israel will allow for cooperation on humanitarian relief to the people of Gaza and hopefully help provide vulnerable populations an alternative to violence. The French peace initiative lacks participation from the two parties, but seeks to find a way back to the negotiating table. It is also worth noting that many from the Israeli security establishment, tired of waiting on negotiators and seeing little leadership from the Israeli defense minister on the issue, have begun to outline a viable security plan for a future two-state solution.

Many have concluded, even among her most ardent proponents, that the most proximate threat facing Israel today is an Israeli-Palestinian conflict that remains unresolved more than 20 years after the signing of the Oslo Accords. The most recent surge in violence has claimed the lives of more than 200 Palestinians, dozens of Israelis, and two Americans, and both Israeli and Palestinian youth are increasingly disillusioned with the diplomatic path. Earlier this year, a devastating terror attack not unlike those that became common during the second intifada was carried out on a commuter bus.

The U.S. has pursued peace negotiations, blocked one-sided United Nations Security Council Resolutions, condemned Israeli settlements in the West Bank, conditioned aid to the Palestinian authority in order to combat violence, and helped build institutions within Palestinian society that facilitate progress towards a negotiated, two-state solution. There is little hope for credible negotiations without a viable Palestinian negotiating partner or governing authority capable of implementing and safeguarding an ultimate agreement. The wholesale defunding of the Palestinian Authority is a misguided approach to addressing problems with Palestinian governance that undermines an ultimate resolution to the conflict.

Despite the lack of recent progress, the U.S. must continue to be seen as a supporter and independent broker of a lasting peace, and on April 8, I joined with a bipartisan coalition of my colleagues to write the President in support of a continued commitment to the peace process. We must continue to search for credible venues and parameters for negotiations, because a great fear the U.S., Israelis, and Palestinians should have is that 20 years from now the conflict endures. Whether it is from intransigence, a lack of political will, or honest missteps, it will be our failure and a future generation's price to pay.